STAYIN' ALIVE IN CHANNEL COUNTRY

To Alec in white roses

Copyright© James Alfred Podhorodecki 2024
Published in February 2024 by James Alfred Podhorodecki
2nd Edition Published September 2025 by James Alfred Podhorodecki

A Stayin' Alive Odyssey
Cover art by Kial Menadue
Typesetting and design by Chris Rigney

ISBN: 978-0-9756385-2-1

All rights reserved.
This book or any portion thereof may not be reproduced or used in any manner whatsoever without the express written permission of the author except for the use of brief quotations in a book review or for academic purposes.

www.wordsofsloan.com

www.kialmenadue.com

James Alfred Podhorodecki MA is a published philosopher focusing on ontology, phenomenology, aesthetics and literature in Sartrean existentialism. He is a writer of Aussie Gonzo Existentialism and has short stories and poetry published by Melbourne/Berlin indie publisher Soyos Books. He is a musician, lyricist and singer, and has released an E.P and L.P as front-man of the Melbourne outfit *Dirty F*. As well as releasing two E.Ps with *Amateur Songs for Friends and Lovers*, an album with *Friends and Lovers*, and an organ instrumental solo single entitled To Wake Up Unsore. Separate to his post graduate research, he is a clinical hypnotherapist focusing on authenticity and existential psychotherapeutic treatment. He lives in Brunswick, Melbourne, and works in a liquor store.

STAYIN' ALIVE IN CHANNEL COUNTRY

James Podhorodecki

Photography by Kial Menadue
Edited by Tom Abraham

Contents

Foreword   11

1. Airports   17
   Mt Isa   26
2. Crabs   31
3. Queensland   45
   A Collection Of Stubby Holders   49
   Pretty Weird But Pretty Good   56
4. Snake Lunches   61
   Everything Is Fake   75
   Fireworks   82
   Eagle Drop   95
5. Whatever, Whatever, Whatever   115
   Camel Tagging   121
   Eggs & Cum   125
   The Rushes   141
   Plastic Chair Republic   157
6. I Am Dysfunction   187
   Back To The Abacus   200
7. Stayin' Alive In Channel Country   209

Foreword

It doesn't take much for a foreword to become skip-over-able. Too long, skip. Too self indulgent, nah. Too intellectual, pass. And so on. Thus, if I'm going to write this thing. Which I already am. And If I'm going to take this space for myself. Which I already have. It's gotta add without taking away.

Like me, James is an idiot . What I mean by that, is he's silly. I've barely read anyone funnier. He writes and thinks with a contagious freedom. I learn something profound about myself every time I read 'me' in his writing. He reminds me that I have convictions. That there's an intelligence earned through action. With my temperament, I can usually offer a sense of levity and buoyancy to the situation. And when its necessary, I'll remind him that he's an idiot.

Stayin Alive is 'us'. The me and him part. Our friendship. Partnership. Accomplice-ship. Image and word. The merging of perspectives, sensibilities, dreams. Go ahead and take those two words from the title - "Stayin' Alive" - and plonk us down anywhere ya like. Stayin' Alive in Antarctica. Bacchus Marsh. The Serengedi. You get it.

But this time it was Channel Country. The name given to an arid, sparsely populated stretch of desert in outback Queensland. Endless horizon in every direction. Sunburnt and brutal. The deserts of Channel Country are a series of ancient flood plains. So if it rains enough, the channels begin to flow. The landscape comes alive like a Sturt Desert Pea. That's what they say anyway. We didn't see none of that. For us, this time, it was all red.

The tiny town of Boulia is out there in the red somewhere. If not for an annual camel race, "Booya" would have surely been forgotten. The Boulia Camel Race. Australia's largest. Thirstiest. The Thirsty Camel Cup. The Melbourne Cup of camel racing. It swells the town of 300 to over 3000 for the weekend. By Monday morning the circus has packed up and left town. Vanished like a mirage.

Depending on who you ask, a significant chunk of Channel Country is known by another name. "Land of the Min Min lights." Home to a mysterious phenomenon that has continued to bewitch a sliver of the Australian imagination since Aboriginal Folklore. Eerie glowing balls that hover above the horizon, beckoning you to follow them, inducing feelings of dread and disorientation. Spirits? UFOs? Fluorescent Gas? Whatever the explanation, the stories are more or less the same, and they all happened in Channel Country.

Reflecting on the experience of this book, I realised we left a few things out there in the desert. The thing we thought we were doing pursuing events. Those ideas had been dying in us for some time. But out there, in the clarity of a harsh new light, they looked as foolish as ever. Like a couple of teenagers who dressed themselves for the formal, its only in the reflection, flicking through the photos after some time has passed, that you can truly see the errors of judgement. *Event* was an excuse to be somewhere. Pre-packaged meaning. A receptive audience. Story and Event aren't in accordance. The story I want to read doesn't start and end with a camel race. Double rums and orange juice at the airport bar, 6am, waiting to see if Victoria will close the border. That's a better place to start a story. That's the story James and I would want to read. So that's exactly where this story starts.

Like jumping into the ocean and feeling the salt concentrate to cuts you didn't know you had, the outback located and exposed a naivety in us. We wanted a project. An experience. An adventure. We asked for a peek behind the curtain at something we didn't understand. We got it. Our dear friend and editor Tom Abraham, half jokingly equates my role in the final chapters of this book to Virgil leading Dante out of the depths of hell. Dramatic, certainly, but there might be some sardonic truth to that. Turns out, things can turn dark pretty quickly out there in the red. Ideas of adventure can degenerate into escape. But even a spectacular failure can elucidate meaning.

Just take this book for example.

Kial Menadue

1

Airports

There's a million ways to start this fuckin thing. And I've been trying my best, the last few days, waking up in sweats, rewriting old prose like a chimpanzee, to re-establish myself and my words, my identity, my writership. What writership? Some false demand I assault upon myself. To be a thing. A fucking thing. The man I'd like to read. The person, the whatever you want. To be a human being that inserts themselves into situations that are seemingly fucking reasonless. Like most of the reasons we do anything at all.

I can't quite get a grip on purpose other than living it through. And I thought I'd stave off the booze and the drugs at least a lil while and yet, 6am airport double rums with orange juice loom outta the atmosphere. And at $42.00 they left their motherfucking dent. Coulda bought a bottle and sipped it mid-flight. "Oh no, you can't do that sir," they'd say, and that'd be fair enough. The oxazepam is doing what it does and had me drifting off nearly after

10 pages into *A Fan's Notes*. I'm done with the impulse of the past heroes. Stop colluding me. Stop chasing me. I don't wanna be you. I wanna figure out who I am. A man on the fringe of society, a god damn mediocrity, a toxic majority, and yet I've nowhere to go, nothing to be, only dreams to follow with words and photographs. At least I have a team. Me and him. And we're a team in our quandary. In our concurrent insignificance. Maybe in the margins of these stupid things we see ourselves. Pointless, but time consuming. Passionately life sucking. Give your time and your desire to a dream - barely a fuckin fart to squeak of. I keep wondering if this one, this one here, so far away from home, riding on our own small change. I keep wondering if this big spend on a big dream makes it all the more real? There's a new maturity maybe... But what do I really know? I know that drugs don't make a story. Insanity doesn't reveal the sane. I know that I have to process this bullshit my own way and not write for journals, publications and that trash. Because they make you theirs. And I have nothing that can be shaped. I can barely shape the shit myself. Maybe in the outback. In a tent. With the mystery of our future and our-selves before us we can hope to glimpse, a shimmering of something larger. The thing we've always wanted, at whatever cost. Friends in arms. Stubbornly experiencing life and loving what we endure of it. Reflecting our perceptions of shit

unknown to a miniscule part of the wasted world. We're tied to this subcultural confusion because that's where we live too. There's no discourse in what we do. We don't even know where we begin. There's no audience. We are the audience and we live it. We give it up and refine it, so that it has some merit, something to be proud of. Something to prove, so that my adventure wasn't just lived but agonized over. But I'd be lying if I said it wasn't for me, and Kial'd be lying if he said it wasn't for him. To throw ourselves into the desert, into a sport we've not a clue about and work it all out. The more we toss our bodies around and the more we bend our visions, the more hope we have of finding reason. We do this automatically, without any reason at all. We know we wanna do this for the rest of our lives. A project or two or three a year. Insert ourselves, discover and comprehend. But there's always me in the way. Always the ego in the way. Always the question of "who the hell are we?" that's in the way. Reveal to me the secrets of self-knowledge and the secret of the written word please, Channel Country. Where else do we have to go to find the beauty in the ritual of subterfuge and recompense? Cause we'll keep going everywhere. Anywhere in the world, and not a single fuckin' piece needs to be published for us to book more flights, rent more cars, camp out nowhere, ride down dirt tracks, befriend rednecks and bigots, celebrate bloodshed, subdue our disgust of animal cruelty etc. etc.

to get to something. I dunno what it is. But it's all worth it. Because there's a story everywhere, and the one within relies on the one outside. The further and more obscure that tale is, those people are, the more obscurities we can ascertain within ourselves. We're not old enough yet to be void of romance. Let it die in all other ways but in the ways of style. Trying to find the best way possible to sustain a life, to sustain meaning. Even if it's through a fuckin camel race, or through ancient folklore lights that position themselves randomly in the dark Northern skies full of aboriginal myth now turned into a tourist attraction. Supposedly these lights, green, red and blue will flicker in the night sky for no discernable reason. The sightings are so common and frequent and have been documented for so long that there's a whole town named after them. But they're likely just fuckin gas, likely there's no mystery at all. But isn't that always the way? The world provides the substance and you add the magic. And maybe someone else sees a bit of that magic too. Or maybe you take it all away. And there's magic in that too.

This looks like another fucking self-righteous asshole chasing the stories chased a million times before step by step, following the manual. But I'm not looking for the Australian dream. I'm not looking for the camel dream. The Min Min dream. The gambler's dream. The traveler's, the drunkard's, or the drug addict's dream. I'm looking for my own. And I thought I found it before. I did find it before. But there's dreaming and then there's living it through - the daylight and the sunburn and the hotness of heat. There's not wincing away from the light once it's burning and bright and that little tired voice is begging you to quit. It's not done until it's right. So, here we go. Try again. Try better. Do better. Be the dream.

After landing in Brisbane we get veg ramen and Asahi from the food court. Country music emanates overhead, dominating the eardrum. It's no good. But why would it be? The Asahi is good. And I take a Centrelink call just before I can sip it. "Sorry I called so late." "No, problems, I actually just landed in Brisbane." "Oh, wow, nice what are you doing there?" "Covering a story, hopefully to get published, hopefully earn some money, haha." "Oh, ok, cool. Still looking for jobs?" "Yeah." "And still a full time Masters? 50 hours a week?" "Yeah, managed to get a pause on it for this, which is nice." "Yeah, it is." "Yeah." "So this for Uni or?" "Nah, for work really. Hoping to be able to publish it, so yeah." "Oh, good." "You've still got 15 jobs to do and get in by Monday, just a reminder. So, we need them in time, just have them all uploaded." "Yeah, yep. That's all good." I haven't done any of them. How am I gonna fuckin do them. This is a drag. "Ok, well, I'll let you go. Good luck with the story, what's it on?" "Camel racing…. There's an event up here once a year." "Brisbane?" "Nah, Central West Queensland, Boulia." "Oh, ok, yeah was gonna say must be really far North." "Yep." "Alright, well goodluck with it." "Cheers man, have a good day." "Yeah, you too."

I sit back down at the lifeless airport bar. Take a sip of the beer. It's better after that. The ramen is cheap. But healthier than anything I'll be eating the next few days I imagine. I look for game 4 of the NBA finals. Kial fiddles with the borrowed camera. He has to get comfortable with it quickly. Four hours till boarding the plane to Mt Isa. And I assume the tense of this story will change dramatically, but you'll have to enjoy that. It'll move from here and now quickly into there and then. That's what happens, I write as the events unfold. Some in the notebook. Other times, like now, it's pouring out directly into document.

There's some fucking country song about skydiving changing this guy's whole life. Looking down at nothing made him think about what it would be like to live like you were dying. I wish I could teleport into the past and put a pin through his parachute just to help him out. Then he could know. Then he could really know. And he'd know real quick, and he'd realise there weren't much he could do with a perspective like his. At best he'd leave a body sized indentation in some freshly mowed grass. And what makes my perspective so interesting? As much as I want reformation and idealism in my text, in my life, in this choice to bounce around to nowhere-lands collating stories and pictures of people submitting themselves to something bigger than themselves. I want the whole scope of this thing to open up like a gaping asshole. A double penetrated rectum. I want to let you all look inside the bowels and the guts of the sluts of ourselves and the whores of our dreams. Whore them out, because a dream is better at work than it is behind a counter. A dream is better burnt out, than it is prim and proper, and my ideas are starting to sound like country songs already.

During a cigarette outside airport confines, the little smoking retreat like an encircled AA meeting, I felt the heat of a sun that was unfamiliar, a sun that had a bit of life in it. And maybe that's all it took, some liveliness, subtle as it was, to bring on feelings from outside myself. And I started thinking about the camel racers when I came back up the escalator and walked past a group of female hockey players. Do the camel racers talk performance? Do they train all year round? Who wants to be a camel racer? In this way I can relate. Who wants to be a whatever the fuck this is? Where's the camel racers manual? Somewhere a little further North maybe. If I get my hands on a copy I'll transcribe a few passages.

Everyone in this airport is overweight. Plump rosy little fatties biting into sausage rolls. Whole sticks of pastry shoveled into one lil old man gob. People sitting around on laptops farting away at their jobs, their jobs, their jobs. And the country music hasn't let up for two hours. I suppose a taste of what's to come. Songs of whisky, trucks, hitting women and Friday night drinks. If you don't ask for more, you shall not receive. If you ask for more... you probably won't anyway. So, I ask for camel races in the desert and mysterious lights that flicker around in the sky like fabulized rainbow floaters in your iris.

Asinine patrons board the plane. The sorts of bodies that don't belong this far South, that far North, or anywhere along the way. Bodies reddened by weather, pallid skin that simply can't adequately protect itself from the relentless outback elements. These people look like the swollen bodies of crocodiles, ankles amassed with fluid ready to burst with the poking of a sharp broken stick. But on this three-and-a-half-hour flight, from Brisbane to Mt Isa, I'm delivered something of a revelation thanks to Exley, and it comes in just the form I've been looking for - hunger. I was told I was a decent writer at 13 by my High School lit teacher. That's all a sad angry child needed to leap from abject indifference to permanent obsession and blind faith. I spent every moment since, thinking I was a natural, because I never really read anything. I spent every day at University reassured of this pompous and unproven belief due to good grades and blunted peers. There is a loosening I feel around the shoulders, and in the throat now, and it comes with realising that I am not fucking good enough and never have been. And my longing to be good isn't a longing for recognition at all, because I believed I already had that, and for those that didn't believe it or didn't see it, well, they were blind, stupid, daft and dumb, literary luddites and philistines. But being told you're good doesn't make you great. It makes you lazy. And I'm unhappy. And I'm unhappy because I long to be great. And I long to be great because I long for my stories to be great. And my stories are my life, there is no separation, none whatsoever. The pale ale I pour down my throat in this chair in the sky between Brisbane and Mt Isa doesn't write stories. My melancholy, the deep burrowing hunger, the suffering of being inadequate does.

* Mt. Isa

Landing in the penumbra of a red sun and shit sets in. The hot heat hits. It's good. There's excitement, it's like a cough - a relief, but over - instant. We call a cab because they don't keep churning through the airport here. Freight trucks rusted like shipwrecks shake my boots flat on the concrete just 100 meters from the dusty highway. The sun is fading. It's the fucking postcard. I'm in some sort of post card and I'm lost in the two dimensionality of my own fears. To write again. To write again. To write better than ever. I smoke a cigarette and think of the guys in the baggage area where the bags pop out quick like toast from a toaster, pop pop pop they pop out, soon as they seem to have been put in, white toast. White toast everywhere. The men are big and the men are white toast. Rugby men all around me. Tattoos of skulls, like bad hoodie designs. UFC t-shirt tattoos all up their legs, over their shaved heads in their mullets. A fucked demeanor. I become unbelievably aware of my stature. My under 6ft frame. My atrophying body and my beer belly. My fine features. My feminine face. Kial's long blonde hair. My boots aren't heeled enough. I'm short here. Fucksake. I'm small here. Will I feel this way the whole time? I smoke a cigarette as the sun wanes. The cab comes and we get to the Abacus

Inn and all the way I'm thankful that I have at least 15 cigarettes until tomorrow because I'm on edge. Not excited. On edge. I don't know anything here, but what did I know at home? Does feeling safe, feeling repeated, give grand delusions of genius and vision? YES! It does.

Check in. I spy the fridge by reception and a six pack of UDLs are $40. Yes. Deep breaths. Deep breaths. Why is somewhere new elucidating such confusion? A moment ago, I was on a plane having a crisis, albeit a familiar one, and now I'm walking to room twelve in dry Queensland heat, stars edging their already dead and pompous ghost faces into view, and I'm lugging bags of superfluous clothing into a tiny two bedded room with brown brick walls and a stone patio to smoke on. Why the tension I'm feeling? Because this is the first time I've left my 5km radius in how many months? Is that it? And Suddenly Susan, I'm here? I don't know. I know this tension must be inside myself because Kial walks with his usual self-assured gait. He dumps his bags and breathes in the hot air. He unzips his camera bag and shows me a UV light he brought in case the Min Min lights theme presents itself. "Probably don't want to shine this around in here, but let's have a look anyway." He gives me a pair of glasses and we look at all the semen that's been sprayed around the room, in the bathroom, on the beds. Surprisingly it's pretty clean.

"When you shine this on organic matter it will come out a certain colour depending on the thing." "Cool." "Yeah, we'll see I guess. Might not need it." He stretches his arms out and grabs his DSLR, smiles, says something contented, and leaves the room to shoot a few things outside. Instead I wash my face in the sink and dodge my own eye contact. I think about changing my shirt because this grey one is too tight and I feel foolish, unmasculine and foolish. Fat. I imagine hearing from a drunk when I'm trying to smoke out front of the restaurant, "What are you doin' here?" and I imagine myself answering, in a thousand ways, ways that don't fit, ways that are dumb. What am I doing out here? I look like a fool. I have absolutely no concept of a story. And it can't just be me. I'm done with just me. I breathe deep again. Soak this shit up and it'll come through you, I tell myself. I'm a coward. Get some beer, get some chips. The menu here is meat only. And chips. Get some beer. Get some beer. Get some chips. But get some beer.

Even standing at the counter ordering I feel my face going red. Am I blushing? The dude at the counter is comfortable, I say, "Chips." He says, "With sauce?" I say, "No." How is he in himself? If he's being himself, where the fuck am I? I feel like he could rob me. Rape me. Pat my hair. And he's not intimidating. He's a fuckin guy at a pit-stop motel tuck-shop thing and I'm more-or-less frozen to the tiles I'm standing on. Weak. A bride. Wedded to ideas that I'm hoping divorce me. Wedded to a self that I hope divorces me. Kial snaps photos openly of the caps behind the counter, just dumb caps, stupid hats, whatever. He plays on his phone. Casual. Excited. Aloof in himself as per usual. Three beers quick. Three beers in 20 minutes. Ok. It's coming back, but remember you said you weren't letting booze write this story? I tell myself. Do you remember anything at all? Never.

Drinking XXXX I realise it's just rinse. That's why I never drink the shit. I smoke two cigarettes quickly by the trickling swamp pool that sits out the front. Running water helps. Always. Every car in the carpark is a 4wd, a Ute or a truck. Everything is shaved back and raw. Refined for its Darwinian purpose. Survival of... for so long I've been just surviving. And now purpose is here. I've flown into purpose. I read on my phone that a five-day lockdown has just been sanctioned by Victoria. As of now. Just now. And we're here.

2

Crabs

Tussling sheets all night, rolling around, front back sideways, facedown, dreams of hermit crabs in a netted bag at a supermarket. I desperately tried to rescue them when the cashiers weren't looking. I could see them trying to reach out their little crab legs, aching to get a leg out, begging, crying with their tiny crustacean bodies, shells knocking against each other and there were shelves and shelves of them. One was loose, I picked it up and saw that its body was lifeless. It was old, had been sitting on the shelf, fallen through some cracks and died. Now a husk. Old and dead, never having seen any life. I found another that had fallen through the cracks, the size of my palm, I put it in my pocket as carefully as I could so as not to injure it or get a leg caught. Then I grabbed a bag, blue plastic netted bag filled with these tortured things and ran out the store and people yelled after me and Fia asked what I was doing. "I have to rescue them! I have to save them. I can't save them all! I can't save them all!" It didn't feel good enough. I emptied the bag onto a patch of sand by a bridge over a creek. It then becomes blurry - the dream fades away. The rescue wasn't good enough to cement itself in my mind as a success. It was still a failure. I saved what I could, but the rest were still in netted bags in that supermarket dying and crushed. Tucked in their shells, unable to breathe or move or stretch out. Suffocating. Waiting to die. They were expecting to die a meaningless life. I woke up unsteady. Then fell back to sleep. And I dreamt again, but this time of falling into brown river water and sinking into sunken buildings. They turned to sand as I sank into them. As my feet touched their surfaces they fell apart and buried me, underwater, in the brown river, and I was pulled out by a pair of arms again and again, laid on my back gasping for air, again and again. When I was laid on the deck of this makeshift raft, I was singing a song that in the dream I thought was a Jack Ladder song, but after waking, turned out to be my own. I had sand on my lips each time I was yanked up. It was the only thing I could feel. My parents and Fia kept heaving my wet sinking body, covered in sogged debris from crumbling underwater buildings out of the water as we zoomed across this river on some kind of motor raft. All I could feel was the coarseness of the sand on my lips. And I kept singing each time I was pulled out. "Oh, the nurse came, gave me my medicine, and made me act like, I was 27." Over and over. Until I somehow broke the relentless cycle, woke up and got out of bed, went to my phone on the motel room desk by the microwave and wrote it down. And there were other women in the dream. The one of significance was Alice.

At sunrise we were up. We showered and got a strong coffee from a plastic machine near the restaurant. I asked the lady at reception to call us a cab to the airport so we could get our rental car. On the way I saw signs I didn't see last night. Big bill boards all advertising the mining industry and the steel industry etc. The woman at Budget car hire was having a shit morning. But she was nice. "I asked on the thing if we could have two drivers?" Kial said. "You's are married arentcha." She answers, smiling. We looked at her quizzically until it registers. Ah, yeah, to save on the cost of the thing. Sure, sure. It's a white Toyota sedan. It'll be just fine. We get in, get the phone bluetoothed and move out. Kial stopped to shoot within a few km of the airport. We drive to town. It's just nine minutes away. It takes just under an hour because we stop for photos. Which is fine, because in the car I write and it gets rid of a bit of post-dream anxiety. The plastic coffee machine made it worse. That and the two cigarettes made it worse. My birthday being tomorrow made it worse. I feel shorter than I ever have. I feel 4"5 and about to shit myself.

We cross the bridge to Woolworths in Mt Isa. As I relay the dream of the hermit crabs to Kial I see two Aboriginal folks sitting cross legged under a gum gazing at a drying up riverbed. And I look over the small concrete bridge outta the car. "This is almost exactly the same as the fucking bridge, man." Kial slows over it, "Fuck, man. This is pretty much the same fucking bridge. The low water, the creek. Fucksake." And, of course it is, whether it is or it isn't, of course it is. We park and get a trolley. Black folks everywhere in bright singlets and thongs, skin like sleeping midnight, skin like a sky without any stars. I'm nicely reminded that this place has beauty, has history, something I've always felt so lacking in Melbourne. There's a deadness there. There's an emptiness, a bourgeoise fuckery. Feels like somehow everyone is in a black turtleneck, and that's fine, I own one. But there's a lot of pretending that isn't here. I wonder if we brought it with us though, the fakery of Melbourne and our insipid inspirations? We stand out in Woolworths. Or it feels like we stand out. I can't shake the feeling that we aren't right here. Whether it's my anxiety from being in lockdown so long or anxiety associated with this forced identity of becoming a writer or just this part of the world, I don't know. The Woolworths is different to any of the ones I've been to before. It feels like it's been built too quick and left to rot. All the fresh food looks plastic, wax covered and opaque. Most of the aisles are filled with junk, chips, cheese covered puff things, soft drink, canned meals, sugar loaded carb filled processed food. It's only adding to the discomfort and anxiety. I'm not sure I feel alive. We get celery, carrots, hummus, Sa-ka-ta's, two 4-liter slabs of water, apples, bananas. I get rolling tobacco. I saw a dollar store around the corner. We follow a stumbling aboriginal man with matted hair and a limp in what looks like his only pair of clothes, stuck to his body like phony war paint. I wanna ask him how he's doing? Where he's going? I don't. The indigenous woman at the dollar store, hunched over, with yellow and red dye in her long black hair keeps calling me "Sir" when I ask her where an eski or something like it might be. I'm not a fucking Sir I think. I'm a puny man and my clothes don't fit. She points to a spot where the eskis used to be and I see a cursive tattoo saying *story* on the inside of her arm. What it means to her I don't know. But her tattoo gives me the first feeling of belonging I've had since leaving home. Except maybe drinking at the airport and on the plane and at the motel because drinking does that too. Drinking always takes me home. We get a plastic tub with a lid, drive down to the liquor store where an Aboriginal fella is yelling at the cashier over the price of Bundaberg and we get a 30 pack of Emu cans, four Turkey 101s and a six pack of Brick Lane draught for the car ride. 300km ahead of us we have only red fuckin red desert. We have red in front of us and a few shrubs, hawks overhead, Tom Waits through the car Bluetooth until the internet connection dies. Red desert East and West. I make a call to my Father. He says borders just closed to Victoria today. We made it. We're here. It's the feeling of not being trapped that's maybe fucking me up. I open a can prior 12pm. I note the time because I'm judging myself, but this is not the time to start counting drinks. It's not. I am what I am what I am what I am. Pull yourself together. You've been here before, in another way, but you've been here before. You and Kial have done this before. We settle into the dirt road and we turn the volume up.

We pull past rocks with graffitied names, bikes in trees and a dollhouse sized cemetery just near someone's driveway that has Slaughterman Creek Farm written on a painted white mailbox barrel. We pull over by the cemetery. It has the essence of what's homemade and home-kept. A small white stool over a grave. Plastic flowers. A park bench with a trampoline skeleton used as a roof stuffed with old rusted steel wire and shrub. The cemetery is like a gift shop for the unused. Everything's meant to last forever around it. The cheap cement, the wooden crosses, the faded flowers that never lived but somehow still manage to wither. Vestiges of care and adornment. A severe and childish loneliness comes from walking through it.

Benches surround one grave. Most middle names are 'Mary' and they're all graves for Indiginous folks. Bundy and coke and XXXX cans weathered and worn in good faith for those lost. No gravestone is set earlier than the nineties, nobody buried here post 2005. Kial takes photos and the wind rustles his cut off white t-shirt sending thin vines of breeze through his blonde hair. The colonised grave is a gristly thing. It feels cheap. It looks dead. Something about trying to keep memories alive that beg to die leave only traces of death behind. I piss on a ball of kangaroo shit outside the cemetery fence. Then we drive on to the next little town.

Dajarra. And there's a bar or pub sign. So, we pull into the town or whatever the fuck it is. Kial walks into what's named the Public Bar feeling a little sweaty and frazzled. "You blokes goin' Booya?!" bellows an acidic baritone voice "you got the app?" he asks. "Nah, I don't," says Kial. "What?" I hear this from the car. I get out because I figure the backward blimp has no idea what he's talking about. He's been sitting in this pub/shed all day, all week, all his life, whatever, serving locals and listening to the paranoia of the radio. "Just sign in mate? That what you mean?" I say. "Yeah, the app," says the cracked man. He's a big man, white but not outta place here surrounded by rusted junk in everyone's yard. "Yeah, yeah, I'll just sign us both in mate," I say and I photo the thing with my phone and the website starts loading. I say mate way too much in these situations. Kial orders two XXXX cans. "Those the full-strength ones?" asks Kial. "Yeah mate! Haha! No worries," the big fella says enjoying the harsh blokiness of himself against our reserve. His beard looks like all the housing around here that's falling away into the rotting heat of the wild wind. Was this his dream bar? It's just a shed. "And two waters?" adds Kial. "Signing in mate," I say, but it doesn't load. "Didn't know if you's blokes was inspectors or what?" "Nah nah, haha." He serves the XXXX. Bloke at the bar, on a stool, old and white haired, old and off, way off, says, "Booya, ey blokes? Go Camel taggin'! They kick any fuckin way they do. Kick ya sideways, frontwards!" "What? From the front?" I say, feigning interest with too much ardor. "Yeah, fuckin from the front, the side, the back. Fuckin go taggin." Then he drops the word 'Boong' somewhere, and I'm off guard and can't comprehend where there was even space for him to insert it. It's spun all the other words outta the sentence for me. "Hey, the internet is shit. I can't sign in." "Worse than shit. It's fucked!" laughs the big fella and the white-haired oldie at the bar gives a laugh and then this woman who's likely the bartender's wife comes out and squawks, "You boys going ta Booya?" "Yeah," we say. "Them camels are wild ya know. In the taggin, wild camels." "No shit?" we say, and the bartender cackles deep from his gross fat gut. "Yeah fuckin, they aren't trained! They're dangerous. You can win a grand though." "A grand?" I say, "wouldn't mind that." I try to get them to understand me somehow as someone who isn't foreign, someone who isn't removed from them, but it doesn't work and neither does my internet. "Internet isn't working mate." I say again. "Well, you'll be taking these on the road wontcha boys?" "Yeah, we will," says Kial. "Then yous can get fucked and get back in ya car," he says. But he says it in a way that jokes, but doesn't joke at all. Maybe he could smell the black-fella blood in Kial's veins despite his blue eyes and blonde hair. Dumb fat cunt. So backwards all there is to do is laugh. That damn weird Aussie sarcasm that says what it wants indirectly by being absolutely fucking direct. In the car Kial tells me he told them he was from Victoria, says he's gotta stop doing that. "Fuck it, man. If they ask, whatever." But now the borders are closed and Vic is locked down there's a stigma. We're infected by proxy. And those folks in the Public bar will likely chat about us - the health inspectors, for the rest of the afternoon. We open the beers in the car and get outta there. We're halfway. Just over halfway.

A grey 4wd dust bombs past us and disappears into plumes of red sand. Fuck. Was that a… We're 5km from Boulia. The 4wd does a U-turn. Red and blue lights flash as it fish tails round. I can't see. I'm fair good and drunk now. It speeds up our ass. "Shit" says Kial. "No way." "Do I pull over?" asks Kial, "Are they behind us flashing?" "Yeah. Yeah, fuck, pullover. Now, ughh… because they were coming at us they don't know our speed, Ok. Just say we were going the speed limit." I tell Kial. A young cop and a burly type get out and smugly meander toward us. The young cop does the work. He asks us how fast we thought we were going. "Ah, I dunno, 110?" says Kial. I wince. "113," the junior says. I've already hidden the beer cans, crushed em and stuffed them in the door. Is Kial over the limit? They have to breathalyze him and I'm over. Definitely over. I've had more than him because he's been driving. I've been blissing out down the trail. But, if he's anywhere near me we're done and I've been passing him cans. They breathalyze him. I look out to the desert. The red road. How do I take over from here? How do we get anywhere? Can I refuse a breath test cause I'm not driving? Do I legally have to oblige? "You know what the speed limit is?" "Ahh, nah I dunno," Kial says. "100," says junior with a chip. Fuck. Other cop looks at the breatho and I hear a disheartened, "All zeros." "Now we're just gonna drug test you, alright?" "Alright," says Kial. The cops walk back to the car and retrieve the drug test. "FUCK," "Yeah, fuck, dude. It's fine. Fuck." We go silent. The cop comes back and gives him the test. He peers down at the little thing and shakes his head. "We're giving you a ticket for speeding." "How much is that?" Kial asks. "$275," he says, "We can email it to you or write it up on the spot, but you gotta pay it within 28 days or there will be a suspension of license." "No worries," says Kial. The cops walk off and climb back in their grey 4wd. "I'll split the ticket with you." "You don't have to do that." "No, I'm splitting it." If I was driving I'd be doing 180 and I'd be over the limit. Whatever we're doing were in it together. It's ours. It's fine, man." "Ok."

We drive into Min Min down as hell. Down and down. And down and down. We cruise around the shithole, doing laps of the tiny square of shit houses. Places meant temporary made permanent. How much was meant to be short lived? We ask the general store for directions to the races cause we can't fucking find directions anywhere. There're no signs, how are there no signs? "Left then a right and you'll see the signs," the little lady says from behind the counter of her shed looking shed sized supermarket. Everything here has been dropped. Built badly. Built carelessly. We drive on, and Kial's pissed about the ticket. We talk it through. He can contest it. It'll be ok. I'm taking half, that's like $135, it's nothing. It's the cost of a ride in the chopper out there. Kial had said that to the cops too, he said, "There goes our ride in the chopper I guess." And they smirked. They didn't give a fuck. We let them down because we weren't drunk and high and we weren't doing 180. Well Kial wasn't. I would have given them everything their priddy blue hearts desired. Turning into the grounds we find a nice spot under a tree not so surrounded by caravans. The old man near us is chopping wood and I ask if he minds if we set up a little two-manner next to him and he says "Not at all," surprised I'd bothered asking.

We set the tent in medium silence. The sun is hot but good. We crack an Emu and we peg the tent in and we sit near an ant's nest for a while under a tree. There's no reception. Can we access the tickets? Fucking hell. We can give a name that'll work at the gate. What are we doing? At least now that we'd set up in a spot we felt a little grounded. Getting pulled over was a blessing. Kial would have cruised into town one afternoon half shitfaced for more beer or to use a payphone or whatever and then we'd have had it for real. He'd have his license revoked and we'd be fucked here in the middle of shitsville. We look around the red dunes and I puff on a cigarette. There're just white people. Everything feels out of place. There's just colonizing cunts. I am displaced. I am an aisle of canned food. I am soft drink. I am white. I am not a writer. Not yet. Maybe never. We drink Emus from the makeshift eski in the boot and eat some crackers with hummus. Then we walk into the track area for the first time, in search of people, camels, events, angles, but more than anything else ideas. Ideas and drinks.

3

Queensland

After our first night, I rolled around in the sleeping bag feeling a few rocks beneath me, nothing unreasonable. Dreams were simple. I awoke unglued from whatever stories were playing through my head. They were narratives. They kept the same part of me that was on all day now on all night. Kial went for a shower. I opened a can of Annalisa baked beans and ate half of it sitting in the sun on a pile of soft dirt with *A Fan's Notes* on the ground beside me. People slowly drifted from the shower blocks back to their camper vans. I read a page or two but focused on eating something substantial more than anything else. Baked beans felt like a treat. Cold from the tin. Did we eat yesterday? When Kial came back I told him I saved him the other half of the can. I stood up and kicked the dirt, twisted my foot into it, shy like a child, I said, "It's the same thing every year. I turn a year older -" and Kial interrupts me. "Oh, shit, that's right it's your birthday!" he embraced me and it subsides some of the baggage that came with the words I was about to say. "Thanks," I said, "but, yeah," I exhale. "It's the same thing every year. I'm older again, and now I'm thinking what have I accomplished?" And we both say, "Nothing," simultaneously. "Every time. It's always the same on this day. I've done nothing." We gather our shit, camera, laptop, cigarettes, whatever. I didn't bring a towel. Kial tells me about the rotted plastic curtains that swing open in the shower block, the hocking of loogies and the sound of old men spitting forcefully into drains. I won't shower today. We take ourselves to the track area. It looks and feels different to last night. There's a barista with a coffee-cart. After we order we wander around and kick the dirt. On the fence we see a sign reading Corrections Facility. We ask each other if this could really be a prison work camp. Is this camel race somehow bound up with a correctional facility? The coffee takes half an hour. We set up and Kial gets around and shoots a bit and I read and I think of writing, until I do, which is right now, which is after the first night here, which is after the first sleep and after the first morning, which is on my birthday. As I drink coffee and smoke a cigarette, I chat with a security guy from Dalby, wherever that is. He earns $21 an hour and he tries not to pay any tax. He has to redo his traineeship every three years and it costs him $1200. He's been working random remote event security for 17 years and wants to move to Melbourne to get more work. He's in his sixties, he seems alone, he has gapped teeth and he's a simple and nice enough man but there's something disconcerting about him. There's some buried gentleness in the way he talks to me. It's weird and I don't like it and his story, aside from being significant for conversation, is not significant at all.

I'm staring out at the track sitting at a plastic table on a plastic chair. On the fence is a canvas sign. A fat frump is leaning against it wearing a T-shirt reading, 'Hey vegetarians, my food poops on your food', with a graphic of a deer shitting on some grass. The frump is standing by his frump of a missus and they're leaned onto the sign like frumps, looking out towards the brightening day behind the track. The sign reads 'Queensland'. But somehow, for the first time, I read it as Queens land. Queen's land? Camel races? Campers. Temp homes made permanent. Maybe the magic here isn't magic. Maybe it's ok recognizing that. Maybe this isn't the mysterious and spectacular trip I'd envisioned. Maybe it's an exercise in humility - a coming to grips with the fuckery of it all and the descent of the human spirit? Or is this the human spirit? This Queen's fucking land. And my question being, why am I here? Not only existential, but physical, begins to throb, surrounded by the most speckled hen looking fucks I've ever seen in my life. These carnivorous cretins, these pale maggot creatures, shit feasters. Animal abusing land rapists. I feel anger. Fucking camel races. And all human land is land for humans, yes, yes! But it's not what you do it's how you do it. It's your style, Buk would say. This style is abusive, careless, wretched, and without repentance. How can I repent? That's now my question. How can I repent? This is all too much. I light another cigarette and think about when I should start drinking today. Then I start writing about last night.

* A Collection Of Stubby Holders

The entertainment had been going for a while by the time we'd wandered, fully prepared and a little soused into the track area for the night. We'd made a few trips in and out. But the evening was there to drink into and meet people and try to figure out exactly where we were. Just prior, we'd sat on a small mound up from our tent where earlier Kial had been attacked by ants. They crawled up his hips and tried to get into his ass. But we found a clean looking spot this time, so we sat, and we talked about what we were doing, which at that point was disarmingly vague. But seeing the sun slope down the earth, leaving traces of yellow and orange and red, deep blue, purple, slithers of green, revitalized something. Listening to the crackle of shit music and 'yee-haws' we shared a Wild Turkey and a cigarette and Kial said, "We should do this every night to reconvene. I feel it helping me somehow." He was right, it was helping, when we looked away from the burgeoning event, from what we didn't yet understand and into the setting sun we found something, we could hear a rumbling of something in our chests. It was dumb confidence that we would figure out some reason for being here. It would offer itself to us. We just had to stay alert and not let it slip past. In the brief silence of that Wild Turkey,

A COLLECTION OF STUBBY HOLDERS

Kial remarked, "If anything, our projects will at least be a collection of stubby holders." I laughed because he might be right. And what did it matter if he was? At the time it felt like it meant the entire world.

When we entered the track area that night the starting entertainment for the weekend was an overheard and obnoxious cover song touted by a Drag Queen. I hear them talking up the audience throughout their hour long set where they covered Kylie Minogue, something by The Beatles, Dancing Queen and a bunch of those cheesy Priscilla Queen of The Desert type numbers. They said to the audience, "Just remember boys, a man knows what a man likes." The wink that followed was seminal and seismic. And they proceeded to make crass and overtly sexualized advances towards the husbands, the young men, the old men, any men. Keeping my distance at the hill I was struck by how they weren't doing themselves any favours or the LGBTQI+ community any favours. Instead they were quenching their thirsty ego in their tight sequined dress and high heels, bright red curly wig and their caked make-up. They were parading themselves as some kind of joke. The joke for these folks being – 'How preposterous it is for a man to be a woman lol!' yeah big lol. And they were laughing, keeling over, slapping their thighs. Chortling at the absurdity of the performer's appearance.

The entertainment was a parody, not only at the expense of their dignity and pride, but of anyone that identified with a drag or cross dressing lifestyle. They were flaunting themselves and degrading themselves for the benefit of the backward and overtly homophobic crowd. The 'singer' could have been spreading at least subtle notions of equality or revealing on some level the deeply human traits that they find themselves in, but they were distancing themselves from their own humanity. And the music was trite. All they had were stupid jokes perpetuating the divide. It was all ego and ego. That's what was pouring out. A stupid entertainer singing stupid fucking music. Why were they here? Not to invite the audience into an experience, but to mock themselves for their own benefit, ironically at their own expense. The crowd lapped it up.

We drank XXXXs. Kial got some pics. I mostly sat on the grass hill and watched a sea of young country folk flood to the stage which was positioned on the furthest side of the first lane of the track. Mums danced with babies, cops danced with kids, young girls grouped together and shook their rumps to a country cover band. It was weird here at night, amongst all this so suddenly. A girl with a bound leg and a crutch was hopping along to the music, things like The Eagles, Powderfinger, fuckin, whatever, I dunno. Trash and trash. I sat on the knoll and I drank tin and after tin until I decided to get a rum and coke which tasted like dishwashing liquid with white sugar. Kial eventually pulled up some chairs. The older crowd was thinning. It must have been 9pm or something. The band was playing and playing. It seemed they'd never stop. "We can't sit here all night." I said, "We should go down into that pit where they're all dancing." I don't wanna dance, but we should get everything we can. Maybe we'll see something. "Nah, you're right. Yeah. Lets' do it, I guess." Obviously, we were apprehensive. There is nothing in a familiar song that could send us to the front of a stage doe eyed with loose knees and wagging elbows to dance in a crowd. There's an old man standing on a knocked over bin to get some vision. Everyone seems pressed against the fence except us. I see at least four girls with asses like melons. And I mean each cheek. I saw them earlier when Kial and I bought a small chips to share. I asked for mustard. They didn't have any, so they poured tomato sauce all over it. I don't like tomato sauce on my chips. But I ate them and caught one of the melon-assed girls, not bad looking, country as hell, blue eyes glowing in the dark, staring at me. Unperturbed by her very obvious gaze, I decided to hold the stare back. It's not often an eyeball locks onto you without blinking unless you're on public transport in Melbourne and it's followed by a "what cunt?" She held it. We walked and I kept my head slightly turned, eye contact connected to hers in curiosity. I pulled away just as I saw her jaw start to drop a little. Jeeze, I'm not used to a jaw drop. A strangely positive reaction. Some crumbs of masculinity returned to me a little, or least the feeling of possessing some sort of prowess that had waned as it always seems to around birthdays. We walked and heard them giggling.

Purple and blue lights are flashing from either side of the stage. The band's sweating and their boots are stomping. Real country. The girls with the melon asses are dancing and I'm not going near them. The girl with the crutch holds it up and waves it in the air. I start shouting, "Hey, can you swing the crutch in the air again?" The lights were flashing all over it. "What?" she yelled over loud twanging guitar. And I realised how stupid what I'd asked was. I couldn't see Kial anywhere. I asked again anyway, "Can you swing that crutch in the air again for me, sorry. To get a photo. It just looked ridiculous. It was great." Her face dropped. She was self-conscious. Was I humiliating her? "Umm, it was kinda in the moment. I don't think I can do it again." She frowns. Her face is soft. Puffy like someone who feeds on a lotta red meat. And she had a melon ass even on one leg. Is it the jeans? What jeans do these women wear? "Sorry, yeah, I get it." There's a pause. "So, what happened anyway?" I ask awkwardly, trying to restore myself. "I tore every ligament in my knee!" she says beaming. Her face lit up with pride. Why is she reacting like this? "Shit, that sucks." She chuckles, "I was about to throw the thing away. I think I'll just piff it into the crowd!" she yells, buzzing. Where does she think she is? The live music on this camel track is like Meredith or something. What on earth is this. "When did you tear the ligaments?" "Three days ago," she laughs. "Fuck. Yeah, well, maybe don't do that then." "I feel fine though!" she explains, buggin' out with so much furious joy and confidence that I had to move away. I slipped deeper into the crowd where a guy was wrapping his arms around Kial and telling him to drink from his bottle of wine. This guy, Marcus, dragged his girlfriend out here because according to his swaying girlfriend he just wants to go on adventures everywhere all the time. He has a wild smile. He goes bounding through the crowd like a Labrador. We see another face, a guy we asked earlier where to get Boulia stubby holders from. He was a cartoon bear of a man. He told us where and said they were $10. He comes up to us now in the crowd almost wanting to hug us though our only prior interaction was for less than a minute. We shook hands instead and he danced into the crowd again. I couldn't tell how many people were there. But it felt like thousands. I stood back from it. I sipped a Great Northern, if you ask for the originals you get a 4.2% beer instead of a 3.5% for the same price. Both are shit.

Standing in the purple lights, off to the side, I saw Kial talking to an indigenous guy in a dirty white cowboy hat. Kial beckoned him, walking backwards down the dirt track into darkness. Pure night. Away from noise, and away from lights. The man in the white cowboy hat followed Kial. They were chatting. I looked to my right as a woman in a long skirt, about my height, standing alone and aloof in a not too dissimilar context to myself shot me a look. I held it like before with one of the melon girls. But this was more formal. Green eyes. Pale skin. I smiled then looked down. She did too. I looked out to the dirt track to where Kial had been a moment ago. He was gone.

**
Pretty Weird But Pretty Good

"How you doing?" "Pretty good and you?" "Pretty good. Pretty weird, but pretty good." "Why weird?" "Well, look where we are. There's a camel race tomorrow." "Yeah pretty weird," she says. She looks at the ground. "So why are you here? What are you doing here?" "I'm doing a story here. I dunno why. I'm just doing a story and working with a photographer, my friend." "Oh, the guy that was over there?" "Yeah, that was him. We're here together." "And that notebook you're holding… is that full of notes?" "It is. It is." We look at the stage. The purple and blue lights flash and the boots stomp in the dirt and we are just a few steps back, but not really out of it. We're situated in the middle. The two of us standing side by side, looking ahead. "And what are you doing here? Why are you at a camel race?" I ask. "It was something to do. I'm travelling around Australia in a camper and I met some people that told me about this so I came. Anything that I hear of I just pack up and go to." "So, you're just travelling around by yourself?" "Yep." "Hmm… nice. What's made you do that?" She pauses… and takes a small breath. "I'm trying to find purpose," she says. I laugh. "Yeah, yeah, me too. I don't think there is any to be found here though." "Why's that?" "We're at a camel race. But, I mean, I dunno. That's what this project is about it seems. Finding purpose. It's like, whenever I find any, I realise it's not enough. It's perpetual." She nods and raises her drink to her lips. The purple light glimmers off her skin, her eyes go greener. "I worked in civil construction for twelve years, and I got to a point where I thought, what is the point of any of this? What am I doing? So, I bought a campervan, I packed up everything, and I left." "For how long now?" "How long have I been travelling? Since March 12th." "Nice. And how long for? Do you know?" "Well, I think I have enough money for three years. Then maybe I'll go back to Melbourne, work again, save up, and repeat." "Mmm…" "Mmm… indeed." "It's my birthday tomorrow, it's really adding to the existential crisis, I think." She laughs. "Well, tomorrow night I'll buy you a drink for your birthday." "You don't have to do that." "Nah, I want to." "Thanks." And we talk for some time. And Kial is gone for some time. Hours maybe. Her name is Katie. And we yell over the music, in the lights, boots nestling in the soft dirt.

"I'm going to get a drink. I'll be back," she says. When she returns I tell her I didn't expect her to, and she says, "Of course. I would have said I was leaving if I was leaving." I nod. She's direct. I shouldn't have revealed myself then. I toe the dirt, and look down. "Would you like to go sit by a fire maybe?" I ask. The words just came out. I didn't know what to say, but I wanted to talk to her. I wanted to discuss purpose, existence, absurdity and alienation, maybe she wouldn't care. But I wanted to talk. "Then we'd have to start a fire, wouldn't we?" In her eye is a spark of light that doesn't come from the stage. "Yeah, we would, wouldn't we?" Unconvinced she was aware of her innuendo, I look at the stage again, away from looking at her. And she says, "Maybe tomorrow. You're here all weekend I'm guessing?" "Yeah, I am. Tomorrow would be good." We watch for a while in silence getting hit by the cover band noise and we talk every now and again and we face the stage and we face each other and sometimes we look down and then she says that she's going to bed but she might see me tomorrow. "I'm sure you will." I say. And she's gone.

I stand back a bit, nearer to the fence where the sound desk is and the band is still fucking going. Where on earth is Kial? I use my last beer ticket and return to the track and the music hoping Kial will come into vision at some point. It's been so long. I see him emerge from the darkness accompanied by the white cowboy hatted man. Kial's patting him on the back and they're chatting. "Kial. Fuck man." "Hey, hey. Got some great shots." He shows me a glimpse of the screen." "Shit, these look great." He introduces me and says, "Hey give him your beer." "Ok, sure." I give the guy my last beer. "Can't have a cigarette, can I?"

asks the cowboy. "Yeah sure." I roll him a cigarette. I tell him the photos look good. He says he rides and breaks in Broncos and then he asks if we can buy him two more beers. Jeeze. Kial says no problem. He's so stoked with the shots he doesn't give a fuck. Apparently, the people at the bar won't serve him. I ponder what the reasons might be and whether there could be any validation to them. By the time we come back to where the cowboy was standing, where we thought he was waiting, he's gone. We stood there with two XXXXs and decided to drink them. We drank them and I told Kial about Katie and he said he saw her, said she stood out, looked different. I said she was looking for purpose and he laughed. We went back to camp and had a reasonably early night, before midnight, and we sat around our neighbour's embering fire. We drank an Emu and we talked and we looked at the clear night sky and all the stars in vision. I told Kial every time I saw clusters of stars like that I thought of cum. They look like big smears of intergalactic jizz. We went to bed smelling of bonfire and not too drunk at all. I thought of my birthday. I thought of Katie. I thought of purpose. I thought of meaning. And I fell asleep.

4

Snake Lunches

The last 1000 or so words pour out in the morning at a white plastic table on a white plastic chair looking toward the track. The announcer crackles over the megaphone about a damper recipe, saying handfuls of this, handfuls of that, pinches of this, and saying there was no real way to know you were making it right. For literally an hour and a half, a fucking hour and a half he dumbly drawled through the megaphones, pissing on about a nonsensical fucking damper recipe. Kial and I looked at each other, mostly in jaw-dropping awe, shakes of the head and the occasional burst of laughter. At this hour, before the camel races, there really wasn't much to take in apart from the heat, the wrinkled faces of swelling white fools and the infinite cowboy hats that bobbed up and down and in and out of vision. They looked like fish caught in a net, piled on top of each other, eating at each other, rolling and tumbling over each other, gawking at the camels being led in rows of three or four by trainers down the dust track. I couldn't see anything but these fucking hats. I remained seated. I wasn't moving. I had a good spot in some shade, a base for Kial to return to after laps for photos. Though unspoken, both of us knew we weren't really going to catch any races today. We had no legitimate interest in them, and the idea that we might start to develop an interest in it was farcical at this point. Plus, tomorrow we expected the finals, so we could get what we needed then. I drank the coffee and I smoked cigarettes until the idea of having this laptop annoyed me. It wasn't so much the persistent 'gotcha werkin' on a Satdee' comments but more the grueling knowledge of the battery life and the knowledge I'd need it again and I didn't bring any charging things down to the track, just an adapter for the car and that wasn't working. I'd need battery, maybe tonight after something, or maybe first thing tomorrow. Definitely first thing tomorrow doing the exact same thing as today. Kial was into starting the days this way too. Slow and under the sun. Equal parts reflective and observant. He kept telling me to keep my eyes peeled for belt buckles and obnoxious pin covered cowboy hats. But at a point his camera battery died. He sat down. "Feeling pretty chill, pretty good. Feelin' good." Ah yes, the oxazepam was cruising out the morning and providing much needed clarity against that strong jittery coffee. "I need to grab that other battery," he said. "Yeah, I need to charge my laptop." We abandoned our perfect spot in the crowd that was now beginning to flood like that ocean trawling fish net. We'd be lucky to find seats again, but whatever. I'd trade my laptop in for my notebook. The parting of the virgin pages would be today, two years exactly since Kial gave it to me. It was handmade. Sloan debossed on the front.

We sat in the front seat of the white sedan. I put my legs up on the top of the open window. In the morning wearing chucks felt right, as it got later it felt better to wear boots. Brown palladiums which I didn't quite love wearing. I'd rather have my cowboy boots, or, I dunno, something that felt a little more me. Nothing was really feeling quite me here, but I hadn't been feeling me for a while now anyway. I admired the red in my white chucks, now chalky and roughened by the wind instead of grime, booze and piss from the city streets. In a way it felt like I was cleaning them of their life at home with some real earth. I watched as an uncomfortable amount of people walked past leading these little piece-of-shit camping companion dogs. Snake lunches. That's all they were. They plod along, these synchronized, all-the-same-looking-campers, wearing Kirkland or K-mart looking bullshit clothes. Plaid shirts, pants, same cheap shit denim, same camper-vanny looking things. Same age group, that half-retired or retired look in their capitalist and christened weather-beaten eye-yolks. Fattish women who lived on steaks and parmas. Men who did the same but downing middies. Why middies? You fucking shits. Why were middies such a god damn thing here? Well, these all-alike nomadic white leather-skinned "Aussie, Aussie, c'mon, c'mons" would trot their snake lunches through the dust and the dead grass so they could sniff and shit and piss uselessly on whatever, just like their owners. We watched and waited for our things to charge, my laptop, Kial's borrowed battery pack, his phone. I'd long given up on mine. Reception was lost an hour out of Mt Isa, so we'd long lost Tom Waits and just listened to white noise and talk-back the whole way here. But, generally it was the sound of the radio scanning between channels to stabilise on something, which it never did. It was all fuzz. There was likely no magic to be found in any of this. It was the absurdity of it. That had to be it. And we should grant ourselves the right to feel angry at this country music camel carnival. There was a resistance in everything. An entitlement. We had to change some deep facet of ourselves and our perception instead of sitting back and waiting for a shimmering mystery to firecracker into the sky. When we'd spoken on the hill last night Kial agreed, we needed to meet the oddity head on somehow. And that felt right. Hemmingway was wrong, he was too romantic. You can't not judge. A judgement is synonymous with experience. A writer judges at every word.

The cans of Emu were something to look forward to when we got back to our camping spot. During our charging station process, which was both the battery of our tools and the battery of our souls we'd neck three beers and make our way back to the racetrack. Passing the camper couples, we'd reach the entrance and a fat security guard that would blend in with the rest of them, scattered like fat black ants trawled in from somewhere a bit more North, a bit more South, a bit more East or West or whatever, or wherever there was just more desert, more tin sheds, more missions turned towns and we'd dump our Emu exports in the barrel upon entrance. Nobody gave a shit how overt you were with your drinking near the entrances so long as you discarded before entering. We walked around and I took some notes and we bought rum and cokes from the canteen/bar thing. We watched those watching the race. But when we were around it always seemed to be in between races. All we could see were the ocean nets of caught floundering cowboy hats, kids drinking cans of soft drink, a handful of indigenous folk that seemed to only linger by the carnie rides. They must have come out here to give the kids something to do. They didn't drink with the rest of the fat outdoorsmen and wives who were also fat outdoorsmen. The kids span round on the rides, and the men and women sat on the grass in the shade, by the toilets away from any action. There were never any indigenous folk at the canteen. There were never any around the track. Maybe they knew enough about this camel bullshit. They must have known something we didn't. Or maybe these events were as backward and racist as we'd been so far led to assume. Did they not serve booze to blacks? Or maybe these folk didn't have enough money to get that close to the track? Maybe if they stayed in vision of the security they were allowed to let their kids go on the rides? The three rides that were tugged out to nowheresville. You don't wanna assume implicit racism. You'd rather believe that it wasn't so. There's so much here we don't, and will never understand. But so far, that woman at the Dollar Store had called me 'Sir' and that fat cunt at Dejarra had sprung the word mid-sentence 'Boong' and the Bronco Buster was forbidden from drinking.

We collected some more drink tokens from next to the bar and bought a couple more rum and cokes. Again, were we somewhere in between races? Or was it over? Kial saw a power point by the concrete floored toilets. Those wide toilets for cattlemen to shit out their bowels full of rancid old meat and stale bread. "I'm gonna charge the batteries here next time. The charger in the car is too slow." "They'll be fine here?" I ask "Yeah, pfft, they'll be fine. Nobody here is going to steal a camera battery charger. It's too peculiar. They wouldn't know what to do with it." "Even just as something to take and sell or something?" "Nah, nah. It'll be fine. When we get back to the car I'll grab the charger and plug it in. That'll be good." "Ok, sweet. Well, for now? hmm…" We look around from the vantage point of the canteen where the view drops off and leads over the grassy hill past plastic chairs down to where a steel barricade surrounds the track. There were some folks sitting on the other side of the track on a grassy hill next to the stage. "Let's head over there. Get some sun, just chill out a bit and keep our eyes peeled." Kial agreed so we walked over carrying ice-cool plastic cups filled with gutter-cleaner tasting Bundy and coke. We ducked under the steel barrier on the other side and walked up the hill. What was catching my eye wasn't exactly what was catching Kial's. I had a story to find and follow. The aesthetic was all on Kial. It was all tumbling around in his head frantically much like my own. Two perspectives finding equal ground. Where's the cross section? Where that is everything should be, surely. My brain was cracking under the sun with the strain of it. And deeply buried, nestled in my heart was the desire to feel valued. That only comes through making it yourself.

Two girls sat together. They stood out for the most part because they were youthful and attractive. Obviously attractive. But they had a vacant outback fog in their eyes like little chemtrails being deployed across their hollow irises.

They sat with their legs outstretched, the brunette had hers crossed at the ankles, the blonde sat with her white sneakers knocking against each other. As we sat down the blonde turned her head towards me, gave me a near wink and a smile. That outback twinkle, like a star, gawked uncomprehendingly, ignorant of the fact all twinkly stars are long dead. Behind the chemtrails were dead little twinkling stars. Shit, ok. I'm gonna get myself in a position where she wants to speak to me. I'm not making the move. I feel an attachment to Katie. Already? And why? Whatever. If this girl, with her stark white outback teeth and her ponytailed blonde hair, totally girl-next-dooring makes a move, I'll go along for the ride. I couldn't tell Kial what I was picking up on because they were too close to us. The sun was coming in, bouncing hard off corrugated tin, steel rails, earrings, signs, belt buckles like tiny balls of vicious light, piercing, blinding, burning. I sip the gutter-cleaner. Looking past the girls into the scattered and bored, chit chattering middy drinking crowd near the canteen you couldn't see shit. Katie could be staring right at us. What if I ruin tonight with this? I talked to Kial nonchalantly about what we could do this afternoon, what the camel tagging might be like, where the jockeys were hiding with their shiny Saturn shirts. But I had my eye on the girl-next-door. She turned back again and smiled. I smiled back. Ok. "I wanna go check out those pens, near where

I photographed that Bronco Buster last night. You wanna come or no?" I looked at the girl-next-door then back to Kial. "Nah, I'll stay." "Yep, alright. I'll, ahh, be back soon I guess." "Sounds good." He started off down the hill away from the crowd.

I lie down and soaked up the bastard heat of the sun. I'm just here with nobody and with nothing to do. After a bit, a few sips, still lying on my back, I sat up properly and flicked my sunglasses down. They were heading over to me. Too easy. "Hey there, do you think you could take a photo of us?" "Uh, yeah sure. My friend's the photographer but I think I can manage." She handed me an early 2000s film camera. I didn't know what to make of it. "Thanks!" she glowed with chemtrail. The reflected light of those bright white teeth shone right through my beady lil eye-yolks, fried. "You just press here, and that's it." "No focus or anything?" "Nope, just press this. It's easy. It's the last picture on the roll, but no pressure." "No, pressure? Haha. Sure, no pressure at all." "No, really." I stood up not without a drain-cleaner sway and thought myself a little silly. "Where should we stand?" she asked. I was hoping she'd ask me. "Over there, in front of that gate," I said. "Ok." Her friend was quiet and reserved, very uncertain about whatever it was her friend was doing. She gave them away even more because if this was just about a photo her body language wouldn't be so guarded. I took the photo. I wish I could see it now. They stood side by side, arms awkwardly around each other's waists against the steel gate with the other half of the camel track in the distance behind them. They came back up toward me. "Thank you so much!" said the girl-next-door. How old was she? 17, maybe 25? Hard to say. Please don't be 17. "I think I saw you and your friend last night." "Oh yeah?" "Yeah, I think maybe I was drunk and saying something stupid to him." "Oh, I'm sure you weren't." She blushed, put the camera in her bag and kept on. "So, where are you from?" "Victoria, Melbourne." "Oh, cool!" The brunette stood about a meter behind her and was sort of swaying around at the hips, doing semi circles, looking at the ground, perturbed by her friend's game, whatever she was putting on. The blonde was precocious. Adventure in her shoes like frustrated little stones, discomfort at every step, and the other, well, she could likely recite psalm 42 which is a good one. She looked like she was waiting for Daddy to marry her off to a trainee minister. "Where're you guys from?" I asked. "I'm from Mt Isa, well I just, like, moved there two weeks ago!" The excitement was a bit much. "And you?" I called out to her friend, not wanting her to feel excluded. "I'm from (insert a one Chapel and two shed town)." "Cool," I say. "She's just an hour and half, two hours from me, so we came here together." "Oh yeah? Hour and a half, two hours? Neighbours." "Yeah! Practically neighbours!! Haha!" Intensity builds. Pitch builds. She's giving me a squirmy feeling. She's hot though. Was Katie this hot? I only saw her in the dark and everything was purple. The blonde girl-next-door stands there looking at me. My anus clenches. She's just fucking staring at me and looking giddy. I dunno what to do. I think I've forgotten how to talk to women. I suddenly have no idea what I'm doing talking to her at all. This is pointless. "Nice, so why'd you move to Mt Isa? You like it there?" "For work! Yeah, it's so good! There's so much to do! Like this... and yeah, like, we've got like every weekend booked up for the rest of the year!!" She swings her drink around and looks at her friend for confirmation. Her friend nods solemnly and digs her toe into the grass. This interaction has me in a whole new type of discomfort. The blonde goes on. Her smile is so wide that I feel like all my thoughts are falling into it. Her big eyes are full of hope like a long hard sip of the communion chalice. My thoughts, ideas, knowings, fall into the abyss of her giant mouth, which in retrospect is really hot. But at the time, it was like talking to a sesame street puppet. She lists three events for the year. "Huh, ok. Sounds like you're pretty busy then." "Yeah! It's crazy!" she says. You're crazy. "So, you enjoying yourself?" she asks. This is petering out now. "Yeah, I mean, it's fine." "Watch any races?!" she almost hollers at me. Her volume goes from a 3 to a 17. "Umm, nah, actually." "What are ya doing here then!? HAHA!" Woah. Geeze. "Well, I mean, that's a pretty good question actually. Me and my friend are doing a project on this. I'm writing it and he's photographing it. We've done a few things, but, I dunno… We felt like we wanted to do this. We dunno what to expect. But yeah. I mean, so far it's been good." "Oh, so, you're a journalist, and like, did ya get photos of the races or nah?" "No, no. I'm not a journalist. It's kinda abstract in a sense, I guess. It's not really focusing on the obvious racing thing itself. I dunno." I saw her eyes get those chemtrails flying over again. Her heart shaped pupils started to melt. Maybe my words fell down her giant mouth hole? There's a wonderful pause. "So, are you guys having fun?" I ask. "Yeah!!" she holds up her drink. "Good. Good," I say slowly. Kial turns up. Timing. "Hey, guys, this is Kial." "I'm Emma and this is Sharon." I don't actually recall their names, but the brunette was surely in the vicinity of a Sharon and the other was in the range of an Emma. "Enjoying the camel races?" Kial asks. "Yeah!" "Pretty weird stuff," I say. "Yeah, totally weird!!" says Emma. I look at Kial initiating eyes of dread. Save me from this conversation I pray. We talk some more. Her to Kial. Me to her. Kial to her. Nothing is really said and my body language is getting more obvious and Sharon is seriously not digging nothing, which has remained obvious since the beginning. Emma turns to

Sharon, gives a big ol' frown and says to Kial and I, "Ok, well, nice meeting you." "Yep. Might see you round," I say. They walk off, down the hill, over the track, through the gate to the canteen and Kial and I lie down on the grass and reevaluate. "That blonde was pretty hot, she smiled at me when we came up the hill, that's why I didn't go with you, but fuck, she was weird. It was like no lights were on, you know. Fuckin weird." "Yeah, I got that vibe from her. Church girls maybe." "Yeah, yeah, that checks out. Plus, I feel like I'd like to see Katie again tonight and not have that one hanging around or whatever, you know. I'm genuinely interested in her I think." "Yeah, she seemed cool. Bit more together than that one maybe." "Yeah, I dunno. Anyway, whatever, who cares. How'd the shooting go?" "Mmm... yeah. I dunno. Looked very different last night. Maybe something. Too hard to tell now. Do you think there's any more races?" "Hmm... doesn't look like it actually. Fuck it, we probably missed them all. We still have tomorrow." "Yeah, does look like it. Ah well, just get em tomorrow I reckon. Today I'll focus on other stuff. All the bits and pieces around the event. Then tomorrow get some of the racing stuff, jockeys and that. I'm not too worried." "Nah, me either. Well maybe we should charge our shit, maybe eat something from the car. I'm starving." "Yeah, bit of hummus." "Mmm, yeah that'd be good. Maybe a corn chip?" "Ooooo yeah." "Yep." We left the racing area, walked back to the sedan. We stopped by the toilets for Kial to take some photos of the carnie rides and I got on one knee and began to write as people walked past me, around me, whatever, and I wrote what I was convinced was the ending of whatever it is that this is. It was as if struck by some kind of plastic lightning bolt, smashed over the head with it, zapped in the eye-socket with it, oh dear Lord did you send me your most bug-eyed disciple to instill in me the great magnanimous power of foresight!? I wrote –

> There are strange moments of vulgarity – an ethos of unknowing. Whatcha don't feel won't hurtcha. And maybe there is a truth in that. But it's still fucked cause it ain't truth that dictates our lives, it's what you feel, it's what you channel. It's your narrative and how it merges with others. This is Channel Country, where nobody takes responsibility for who they are, who they affect, or anything, nearly anything that ever happens. And I write this drinking on one knee by a children's carnie ride as that red hot sun sinks once again, and I'll never get used to seeing it sink like this. But I know, everywhere on earth, it's sinking… just different.

It now reads like a Bundy commercial.

* Everything Is Fake

We walked the longer way home exiting through a different gate. We watched the chopper land, an expedition we couldn't afford thanks to the local swine. Kial took some shots of a van covered in stickers that I thought to be collected on Ebay. Stickers as representatives of each lil shithole town across this country. "Look where's I been!" I wanted the van to be a lie. But it wasn't. I mean, sure it might me, but probably not. It had gassed-up and left useless and inconsequential traces across the land. The whole country. It had its rape badges. But how much better were we? As the orange started to bleed into the sky we arrived back at the tent, pulled some Emu Export cans from the boot and stuffed them into the $10 stubbie holders. Steep, but everything was out here. Even conviction came with a heavy price to pay, and maybe it should, maybe that's the point. We had two of four Turkey 101's left. "Let's go for a walk up there." Kial pointed at a large mound about a third of a km toward the setting sun, further past where we confided the night before, where there were no camper vans, trucks, cars, anything. It was secluded and insignificant from here, facing the void of sweet chromatic sunsetting nothingness. Last night's conversation on the mound felt good. To reconvene was important. There was so much nonsense experienced during the day. Nothingness nonsense. All you could do was walk around and soak it up. But how did that feel? And what did that mean for my story and for the photo project? What was revealing itself to us? Were we getting any closer to a tangible idea? Kial was right to want a higher and more distant perspective. "Yeah, cool. We'll share the one Turkey?" I said. "Yeah," I finished my beer and replaced the contents of my stubby holder and rolled a few cigarettes to smoke up on the mound. Kial would have one with me up there, we'd share one, like last night. He granted himself one, or really, however many cigarettes he wanted at any given time, but he needed a pleasant moment to make the smoky suicide worth it. He didn't smoke every day. Not every week. Not every month. An element of us was dying here anyway. We hoped another would come alive in its place. We walked toward the sky, over the dry dirt and scrub, crunching the dead sticks under our boots.

The world fell off the edge of that dirt stretch in front of us as we walked in awe towards the resting sun. We realised the mound was a part of a motor-cross track, a pretty big one. We hadn't heard anybody using it. We walked up embankments and down hills tracing some of its course, barely talking but I was thinking of Alice, and why she was in my dream and it dawned on me that I never liked sunsets before her. I never liked sunrises before her. She taught me how to love them. She showed me how to submit to them, so you'd feel something. I learned through her. And here I was, now, in some land of only setting and rising sun. That's all that seemed to happen that was of any value. Everything in between was mutated and fragmented. And maybe her girlfriend in my dream, who was a sort of ice-cubed abstract artist reminiscent of Julian Moore in The Big Lebowski, who I felt I couldn't understand, was representative of my inability to appreciate sunsets and sunrises and beautiful natural things through my forced art. And my sinking, maybe that was a part of me I needed to appreciate, instead of letting myself sink amongst falling buildings I should have been cruising along the surface. In the depths were just cities lost and decaying. Civilizations that no longer mattered, drowned. Before I met her, I didn't understand how the sunset could imbue people with a sense of elation. Walking to the mound, there wasn't much to say. The days would take a piece of you each time. And somehow, the night would give a piece back, whether it was the same one or not was difficult to say. The mound was about two meters from the ground. We walked up the incline and sat on the edge facing away from camp, from the handful of dust-jointed rides, from the spitting camels, the soft dirt track, the concrete canteen, the ocean nets of cowboy hats, the meat and the meat t-shirts, the camper vans, the camper van synthesis that happened to everyone with one, camp fires, snake lunches, the squawking megaphones, the country music, the fucking country music, the church girls, Katie, everything, what felt like was everything. And we took a few deep breaths. "So, you going to read me the ending you wrote?" asked Kial. "Yeah, you ready?" "I think so, yeah." So, I read it to him. "Mmm shit. Yeah, I think read it again. There's something in there," he said. "I think I'll change the watcha, hurtcha and ain't parts. They don't make any sense, anyway." And I read it again and he liked it. And it felt better. It felt fine. Then we really took a few deep breaths. Then we started breathing, big meditative breaths. I turned to Kial. "Turn to me, let's try something," I said, so he did. We faced each other sitting on top of the hill in the shapeless sky and we took three deep breaths each and we slapped each other on the heart in turns after the three breaths and we repeated a mantra. "You're perfect, you got this." "You're perfect, you got this." "You're perfect, you got this." Breathe in and breathe out, breathe in and breathe out, breathe in and breathe out. "You're perfect, you got this." "You're perfect, you got this." "You're perfect, you got this." Breathe in, breathe out, breathe in, breathe out, breathe in, breathe out. We said this together, in unison, we were in this together. Whatever this was. We felt each other's crises. We didn't know what we were doing here. We were just here.

"I've felt so fucked since we got here, man. So aware that I don't belong and so on edge. Everything just feels so fucking out of place." "Me too, from the moment we got off the plane. I've felt so strange. On the defensive." "Yeah, really? Shit. I thought it was just me." "Nah, nah, nah. I've felt like everything's coming at me." "Yeah, I feel like everything is such an imposition, our presence, everything." There's a silence in the sky. "But you know, I think I'm at least figuring something out. Nobody fucking belongs here. Look at these swollen white morons driving through the desert with their polluting campers and their stupid little snake lunches and camels imported from Afghanistan. It's like nothing here is meant to be here. And because they're all in the same absurd boat, the cowboys and all of them, they look at us like we're freaks, but they're the fucking freaks, man. We don't belong here as much as they don't. But at least we're aware of it. They take some sort of sick possession of this event and the outback and this country. And we feel fucked because we stand out. They don't realise all their bullshit stands out too. The camel racing is ridiculous. It's fucking stupid man and all these people are fucking stupid too. I mean, we feel our displacement. I think that gives us the opportunity to utilise it, make amends with it, or transform it into... something different." We passed the Turkey back and forth. "I think it gives us some kind of right to go on the offensive." I said.

"Yeah, fuck! You're right. Fuck them. I'm going to start getting right up in people's faces with that flash. I have to. It makes sense now." "Yes! exactly. Get right in their face. I've been wanting, I mean, we've both been wanting to find something magical. But fuck that, there is no magic here. Everything is fake and nothing belongs except this setting sun. And the fact that we are looking away from it all and formulating some kind of introspection toward this, this view, this nothingness is representative of something! The fact we can find some sort of meaning away from it all, well, this is the only place we're gonna find any magic." "Yeah, you're right. I'm going to change this whole thing." "I mean, even those shots you were taking before, of the carnie ride lights, I knew they were gonna be good." "Yeah, they are good, they felt really good." "Yeah, I know they did. I could feel it. It's because of the falsity of it. They are stupid fake lights and the Min Min lights are just gassy deposits that form in certain temperatures and they've named a whole little shitty town after them. It's not that there's no beauty in them, but that in knowing the falsity of their mystery we can really appreciate the magic of it, the absurdity of it. And that's a weird kind of magic, I guess." "Hmm..." "There's just something in this deception. The fake bullshit and fake people. You know, like that fat red-faced fucker from the Public Bar with his Aussie way of saying things that foreigners always think makes

Aussies so nice. But they don't understand the undertones of it. The undertones are overt. I mean there aren't any undertones at all. Australians are just great at saying unkind things without being direct. Everything has this element of pretending to be something it's not, something it shouldn't be, something misrepresented, misunderstood."
"Yeah, fuck. You're so right."

I took to writing and Kial wandered some around the mound taking photos. Maybe the magic is the letting go, like looking into the sunset, the removing ourselves from obstruction. Maybe it's the ability to absorb, but at events like these, if there are any like these, the absorption becomes impossible because everyone's in their own personal hell. Maybe to hate is ok, to critique is right because it's a facet of reason. It should be used and used well, and beauty is all the better for it. Sunsets are all the better for it. He sat back down and we passed a cigarette back and forth. "I really couldn't think of a better way to spend my birthday. Even though I have no idea what I'm doing here. I never really do this time of year anyway." And we hugged. And the colours in the sky stretched and dissolved into a deep deep purple and the stars were there, and the moon was there, but the moon was always there, always somewhere all day in the brightest bluest sky, the moon drifted, well aware of its position in all of this. Fucking moon.

✳✳
Fireworks

A few Emus were necked before we wandered down to the gate. The beers went down in minutes out here. 375ml cans are poured directly down throats and into stomachs where they'd wash around cool and foamy. Our main source of sustenance. Even so, we could feel our hungry bodies eating themselves. The calories in the hummus were minimal. "Hot chips tonight?" I said to Kial as we walked past the deep-fried food stands, the pizza express truck, the several iron pots of meat that stewed away in a row behind the canteen stirred by a hoard of gangly faceless cretons. "Definitely" said Kial. "Keep an eye out for Katie. I'm not sure I really remember what she looks like, I can't really remember." "How would I remember then?" "I dunno. You seemed to have seen a few glimpses of someone you thought might have been her this morning?" "Yeah, but I dunno if it was." "Alright… I feel like she's worth talking to for whatever reason. Meeting someone who is searching for purpose in a place like this just seems so right, you know?" "Yeah, nah, for sure. I'll let you know if I see her." We got drink tickets. It was the most important thing to start with. We'd been drinking since just before midday and now the night was taking over. The drinks were necessary boosters of morale.

A country band had started playing on the stage. Kial plugged his borrowed battery charger into the wall near the canteen. We held two drinks each and sat on the grass and watched the spectacle of people on the camel tracks dance parochially in the dust. "Let me know if you see any spurs" Kial said. "Yeah, good point. I haven't seen any yet." The drinks went down good and we got more. Nowhere else on the planet will I gratefully drink XXXX and Bundy and cokes.

"I guess we should repeat last night in some sense. I mean, go down there where people are losing their shit and get into it a bit." "Yeah, keep an eye out for glittering shiny things. I dunno." "Yeah, gotcha." We lean against the steel fence and watch the crowd. The band had their own banner behind them in the shed. They're older than last night's band, maybe somehow more professional or something, but who's to say. Not me, it sounds the same. It sounds similar, covers or not, I couldn't tell. "Hey there birthday boy." "Oh, Katie. Hey, thanks. It's good to see you." "You too. How bout that drink later?" "Yeah, for sure. Thank you." "Hey" says Kial. She says, "Hey" back. Then Kial focuses his attention away from us and towards something more interesting, more integral. "So, have you found purpose yet?" I ask. "Ha, no, not exactly. Not in one day." "You don't say. Well, I think it's pretty great what you're doing. It takes some guts you know, to drop everything and just do what you feel like you need to do. And alone too." "Mmm thank you." Her eyes are blue tonight. Not green as I remembered. In these lights they glimmer and they get the sides of my mouth twitching upwards. It's hard to suppress a smile. She is attractive, for sure, and more than that church girl from the hill. And I'm speaking to her. Can speak to her. That's probably all I need. Someone new with something to say. Time exchanging. "I'll get you that drink," she says. "Ok, sounds great." I turn to Kial, "She's getting me a birthday drink, so, yeah, I dunno. I'll be back later on or whatever." "Yeah, easy," Kial says, looking off into the starry distance past the band. And Katie starts off, walking stridently through a gathering crowd toward the canteen. I follow. "Fucking hell, this line is insane." "Oh, I'm sure it'll go quickly." This is the first time I've seen her face in proper light, under white lights, unflattering lights, and still the shape of her face is nice, her eyes almost painfully blue. It's hard to look at anything else. I'm beguiled by these fuckin jewels in her face. I wasn't thinking about sleeping with her when we were in that line, we just talked. I wasn't thinking much at all. I was figuring out a feeling. A feeling of comfort, of desire. It's a simple thing really. It feels nice to spend time with her. This makes sense, in terms of feeling. Whereas nothing else does right now. "You know how everyone down there is dancing and they're getting stimulation from that, and the music? I kinda need conversation in that same way. I require stimulating conversation in order to relax," I tell her. "Right, well maybe you need to do more of what they're doin. Maybe they're onto something." "Yeah. I mean I get it. I get the release of just dancing. But, I can't just unleash and let go for no reason, or to this kinda music you know." "Right, so a big lead singer like you, what did you do when you were in a band? You just stood there?" That's right. I told her I was in a band at some point last night. Dickhead. That's the cheapest move. "No, ha, no. I mean, I moved a lot. I danced in a way. But, it's more the music. I've got to enjoy the music to let go. And it's gotta give me a feeling." "Hmmm." She judges me with that comment. She judges me judging everyone else. I'm evaluating it. Life isn't just a big subjective conquest whereby one comes to terms with the things they like and the things they don't. Sure, some things are ok, some things are great, and other things are fucking bullshit. And this modern-pop-country music is fucking bullshit. That has been established.

"Oh, I love this song!" she says. "Huh? fuck I don't get country music. I just don't get it." "You've never heard this song?" "What? No. How would I have heard it?" She laughs. She looks at me and starts dancing. I stand in the line in my navy trench coat. It's cold. I stand there and look at her in her long thin desert orange skirt, in her cowboy boots, her white singlet, tanned skin. I watch her dance for me. Or for herself? She takes my hand and makes me twirl her, under this light, in this line of people, what is she doing? "C'mon!" she yells. "Uhh, yeah. Fuck. I dunno. Ok." I try to bend my knees or something, I twirl her again, and again, and then I realise that's the only thing I know how to do at about the same time she realises that's about the only thing I know how to do too. "You needa lighten up!" she yells over the crowding cowboys and hoots in the drink line. "Yeah, maybe, I'm too heady" I yell. "What?" she shouts. The cowboy hatted woman behind the counter now screams out to us to come get our drinks. We're at the front of the line already. "I said, I get inside my head too much sometimes," I shout as I walk away from Katie to a different drink slinger. She can't hear me now. I get two Bundy and cokes and two beers and stuff the beers into my pockets.

She's waiting for me in the corner near a big steel pillar that holds up the roof with plastic chairs scattered around annoyingly so you have to 'excuse me' past people whenever you want to leave the canteen. This little blonde thing with huge eyes, blue like everyone's here it seems. Like a puppy she runs at me and grabs my arm, "Harry Potter!!"

"What?!" "You look like Harry Potter." "What the fuck are you saying? No, I don't." "Yes, you do! You DO!" she's giggling incessantly and giving me crazed pupils, bouncing bubbling pupils. Is she on pills? No, I don't think so. She's just around 20 or so and drunk and loving whatever it is I'm doing which is trying to balance some drinks and having brown hair and a long coat. "I don't look like Harry Potter. And I fuckin hate Harry Potter. That's like the worst thing you could've said to me." She laughs, completely unperturbed. "But you do! You Do!" "Errgh." Katie comes up beside me and the girl walks down the hill and keeps turning back to laugh and throw obscure flirtatious smiles. "That girl was saying I look like Harry Potter." "Right," she shrugs. "Yeah, I hate Harry Potter. "Why?" "Cause it's shit." Katie laughs and starts walking with me and asks, "What were you saying before?" "Oh, I get too inside my own head sometimes, sorry about that. I guess. I dunno. Whatever." And this time when I say it I realise I don't mean it at all. It's not the case. It's just that down there in the dismal country pith of this place is a swamp of people that will dance to anything that recalls a beat and rhythm and lyrical content or anything that they've heard before in their past, their childhood, the radio. It's all synonymous with itself only. It's the same old thing. This music. Country music, this country music, is about Friday nights, whisky, beers, women, trucks and tailgating. And every chord progression is the same. It's all the fuckin same. How could anyone get into that? I'm not in my head. I just happen to be thinking. "I think I misread you?" she says holding out a vodka soda. I see her looking at the two rum and cokes I awkwardly balance. I take the vodka soda in the other. "No, no. Usually I'd never drink this. It just seems right here. I dunno. You actually picked right." And I think about what she might have meant by misread me? What does someone's presumed drink for you represent? Well it represents a lot, but before I could figure it out she says in her wet barnyard voice, "I guess you don't wanna go down there and dance eh?" "Well, I mean, not really. I'd rather have a cigarette." "Ok," she nods assertively. And I wonder if she'll follow me and she does. We get to the smoking corner near a gazebo and we sit. She lays out a scarf/blanket/shall/whatever you wanna call it. Enough for two to sit on comfortably. "That's nice. You just have a whole picnic blanket in that bag all the time?" "Yep! Or in my pocket. You can wear it as a scarf, use it as a knapsack, a picnic rug, tie your hair with it. Anything you want." Her eyes light up. "Cin Cin," I say. She laughs, "Cin Cin." Her laughter makes me think I chose the wrong words, but it's the celebration I've come to know. I guess it's 'cheers' around here. We sit back, and get comfortable. It's a bit cold and it's very dark. We hear the country music thwapping its dirty country dick in the shed. "You want one?" I ask. "Sure. I quit smoking a few years ago." "Oh, shit, well maybe I shouldn't be enabling you." "Nah, it's fine. I just smoke when I want now." "Well, that's good. Very good," I say, and pass her the rolled cigarette. "That was quick." "Yeah I know." I roll myself one. "I know I've said it, but it's pretty intense getting a camper and just going around by yourself, it's crazy. I respect it." "Well thank you, my mum made me write a will before I left just in case I died. Mum thought I was going to die. But, look at me, still here, alive," she shrugs in good humour. For some reason she tells me about some of the things in her will and I don't really listen. Maybe because of the music, or the drink I was drinking quickly so I didn't have to deal with possessing five at once, or maybe those fucking blue eyes that said nothing at all to me but allured me anyway. I found myself tuning out, listening, nodding, smiling. I realised what she was saying was losing me somehow. It wasn't that her revealing herself was uninteresting, it's that she was finding a way to give nothing away in doing so. "So, I had to see a therapist before I went away, that was part of the deal. Write a will, see a therapist, mum said. So, I did. And I know a lot of people say it's stupid or unnecessary or whatever, but it was actually fantastic." I'm wondering what age she is from. Nearly everyone I know has seen a therapist. "What? Who says that? That's insane. They likely need therapy the most." I say. She laughs, and I ask, "But it helped right? Or is this purpose thing? This travelling the helping part? What happens when you feel totally alone in the middle of nowhere? If you don't mind me asking?" "No, it's fine. I mean, it can be hard. But, I can always talk to people. It's good to sort of face things. I've spent a lot of time not wanting to think about certain things and I have to sometimes out here, and that's good. I mean, I haven't felt like I needed to call my therapist once since I've been away. And I know I can at any time. But I guess this is working for me." "That's good. I mean, yeah, I've been seeing a clairvoyant since I was 16, so, that's a sort of therapy. I've tried psychologists and psychiatrists in the past, but they never worked." "You what? Wow, I figured you to be very scientific minded. I wouldn't expect you to think that there wasn't an answer to everything." "What? Really? No. I mean, in a way. It really depends. We need science obviously. I just don't think it can help us on an existential level… anyway, whatever." "No, I'm just surprised. I guess you're the tortured artist sort of guy?" "What? No. It's just that not everything has an answer you know. We can't comprehend it all." "No, we can't," she reiterates. We look at the stars, and she says, "I've been tryin' to learn constellations whilst I've been away. What star sign are you?" "Take a nice long drag of that cigarette and take a guess," I say. She exhales but remains confused. "Cancer." She laughs. "You're Capricorn? January 8th?" "Yep, I told you my birth date last night?" "You sure did." "Well, I don't know cancer, but, I know the Virgins, and Sagittarius and another one that I can't remember now." She points at the wide-open sky, "So, you start from the Southern Cross." "That's not a constellation?" I say. "No," she laughs, "But it's easy to start from there." She draws me the virgins and I fuckin dunno what she's drawing and I keep asking her how that makes this and this makes that etc. And she keeps trying to show me but I can't get it. "You know, I wrote the ending to the story today, I think." "Your whole story of the races?" "Yeah, the experience. Well I think I wrote it. And I think, maybe it'll make things make sense. I'll read it to you if you want?" "Yeah, I'd love to hear it." "I don't have it. I left my book in the car this time. I didn't want to have it with me all night again. So, maybe by the fire later?" "Yeah. That sounds good." We laid further back onto her blanket thing and we look up again into the constellations that she knows, into the ones that I don't, into pinholes through the fabric of the dark and cold universe and into its deepest most morose delivery of our own reflection, though I suppose, marred by its lack of nuance, lack of definition, lack of detail of our own subconscious, our own systems and our own actions seem to become a void in it. But it's through this void that we really perceive our reflection, only through nothingness can we really… And then a giant red glowing beam of light shoots across the sky, whistling soundlessly before spraying bits of white and yellow light on either side of it as it coils through the nothingness then bursts into several other tiny sparking white and yellow fiery explosions that crackle and rain down the sheath of empty blackness. Then another. Wail and bang and burst. Another and another. "Holy shit. Are you fucking kidding me!?" I yell. And Katie is clapping and she's laughing and I'm laughing. "Well, this tops it off. It felt good that I wrote the ending to the story today and saw a perfect sunset with Kial. But holy shit, fireworks? On my birthday? I've never experienced that before. This is crazy!" I yell to her. She turns and she smiles at me, and the crackle of fireworks light up those blue eyes and I smile back. And we turn back to the sky commenting on the magnificence of it all. And I tell her when I was a kid I used to hate fireworks. "Why?" she asks perplexed, revolted, disturbed by me even. "Because everyone was just meant to like them. And they're just shot into the sky for no reason, and they exploded and whatever. They did nothing. They were always pointless. Mums and dads and kids gathering around to watch these stupid controlled explosions. I hated the spectacle of it. How it was just assumed everyone would love it, should love it." "You're so cynical. You can't let yourself enjoy anything, can you?" "No, I enjoy them now. Sometimes, I mean, now because I never saw this coming. And this is wild, this makes no sense. It's great. It's a surprise. But as a kid, you know, you don't get a choice, you're just supposed to blindly love them. Anyway, I'm over that now. I can appreciate them." I said. But I knew that wasn't true. Fireworks were still fuckin stupid. But when they sprang out of nowhere like this, on your birthday, then there was something that could be appreciated about them. It's less about them and more about the moment, of where you are, of who you're with. It's like sharing a cigarette. "You know, when I wrote my will, my mum made me organize my funeral. And I said I wanted to be melted into a liquid, I don't want to be burned into ashes. I want to be made into a liquid and then shot up into the sky with fireworks. And then I can land anywhere and have no tombstone or anything." "No, way? What? Like Hunter S. Thompson?" "Who?" "What? Seriously?" "Yeah, I don't know?" "For his funeral he was shot up into the sky with a million dollars' worth of fireworks." The fireworks are still ripping into the sky and we gasp every now and then, as they sparkle and spread throughout the night. "Oh, what? So, it's not original? Damn it." "No, no. You're in good company, believe me. Have you seen the film *Fear and Loathing in Las Vegas*?" "Yeah" "Ok, well, you know the writer that Johnny Depp plays?" "Yeah"

"That's Hunter S. Thompson. He was a political commentator, but he covered these weird whacked out stories like racing in the desert and the American dream." "So, you could say you're doing the same thing? He's like your idol?" "Well, look, I mean yes and no. I think it's important to kill your idols. Reject them at some point. But, I mean, yeah, I'm unsure I'd be writing this story if I weren't at least inspired by him, that's true. Look, anyway, you're in good company. To be shot up into the sky with fireworks for your funeral on your own volition and not through copying him says something. It's good." "Yeah?" "Yeah." And we watched the rest of them boom and split and spread and sparkle and rain and crack and bleed their effervescence into the vast plentitude of sky and sky and sky forever on. And I felt good in her company. And I felt good just there, just talking and I thought she was good. A good person. A different sort of person. And I felt good again, like on the mound, but different here, a little different, but that same kind of good I felt on the mound knowing that it was my birthday and I was feeling something, seeing something special. It felt good to think that things were and could be special.

***
Eagle Drop

After the fireworks I felt a cool silence in myself. It felt like something fatalistic. A disturbed quietude. I was confused by everything that had occurred. Just then, just before, just now. I didn't want to keep Katie out here, in the dark away from the country music and the fun. I felt like my melancholia was a lot of what she had been avoiding, a lot of what she wanted to escape and here I was, bringing it all back. "You wanna go back in and dance?" I asked. "Yeah! c'mon let's go." I chugged the vodka soda and put the dead beer cans we'd used as ashtrays in the bin. We walked into the crowd side by side and I scanned for Kial. There he was holding a cardboard container of cold chips. "What have you been doing?" "I was photographing the fireworks and trying to hold these at the same time." He passed them to me. They were cold and soggy as hell but they were good enough. Katie walked in toward the dancing crowd and I hung back with Kial. "I spoke to some young girls about the Min Min lights. They were telling me there was a fishing hole I would love." "What?" "They asked me if I liked fishing. I said not really, and then they said 'there's this fishing hole that YOU would love'. That I would love? What the hell is that?" "That's fantastic. Maybe you would?" "Yeah," he says sarcastically. "Well I just had a strangely perfect time watching the fireworks with Katie. It was so nice. It felt like they were for me. Fireworks on my birthday, man. I can't believe it. Surreal. The experience was surreal." "Mmm that's good." He says. I eat the rest of the cold chips and we move into the crowd. I see Katie and head towards her with Kial. She smiles. I smile. It's strange that there is no sexual thing going on. I should have felt compelled to kiss her earlier or her me. But I dunno what is happening here. I like her. And I get the feeling she likes me. But something is stopping her, whatever it is. Whatever. I'm not after anything. This whole thing is weird. And that's enough. It's more than enough. It's perfect. The same girl from near the bar bounds up to me out of the dust cloud crowd, yelling that I look like Harry Potter. She points and runs up to me like she knows me. Kial is talking to Katie and this girl is in my ear. I can feel her breath. Her eyes burrow into mine. She's trying to possess me. She wants me. It's so clear. What the hell? She has no leash, no weight, no nothing. Not in the church girl way. I'm off guard. It's satisfying. She practically talks into my mouth, looking up at me, holding me by the arm, then around the waist. Jesus. I look back to Kial and Katie and they're just looking at the stage. The dumb country band playing their horse saddle shaped asses off. Katie didn't give me any resolute impression she wanted me more than in conversation and company. There was no indication I was anything more than someone to interest her. I didn't feel any sexuality or lust from her. And I was wrapped up here in the crowd by some blonde youthful erratic and energetic thing. She was practically salivating. But there was something else going on. This was too sudden. Nothing is so clear cut. "Stop with the Harry Potter thing, please. It's seriously the worst." She laughs big. "But you do!" Then she spurts out, "Are you bi?" "What?" She pulls me by the waist even closer toward her, "Are you bi?" "Umm... what? Why?" I say again. "Are you?" Yeah." "I knew it! As soon as I saw you I could tell!" "Well, I mean, it's just a connection thing. I dunno. If there's something there then there's something there, ya know? I don't care." "I knew it," she says. "Do you wanna kiss me?" she asks. "What?" And she pulls me tight. My eyes scan everything around her. Something is off. Her forwardness is redolent of an agenda. What is she doing? "I think you're with that guy over there aren't you? That dude in the cowboy hat?" "No, no. I don't have a boyfriend," she says in earnest. "Yeah, but, you're obviously with him." I can tell because of their distance and the way his back is directed at her. Some part of him is keeping tabs. His body language is leaning toward her and scanning her, maybe just with the heckles on the back of his neck. But it's happening. "No, he's a friend I've had for years and he's always wanted to be with me but that won't happen." Fuckin' knew it. "Right, but he wants you. And you were dancing with him? You're with him. So, what are you trying to do here? You're playing a game with him. So why?" She bursts out laughing, "No. I'm not!" She steadies herself to me and leans upwards, so I lean down and her lips brush against mine and mine against hers and she opens her mouth and my lips press to hers, and she closes her mouth a little and I follow, then I open my mouth more, opening hers with my lips and I dart a tongue around, just a little, and her tongue responds and then she pushes me away and bursts out laughing again. I smile. "Alright," I say, and she dances against me a bit, then turns her head to the kid in the cowboy hat and he's watching the band, or maybe he saw with his heckles, just like she wanted him to as her ass pushes into my crotch. She laughs at me again and then turns away and yells out to some friend she's with that I look like Harry Potter and her friend smiles and shrugs. "Fucksake," I say. "I want to make out with him," she says to me, and points to a tall guy, a big guy. "He's got one eye, but I don't think he wants me," she says into my ear. "Right, well, go make out with him. He's got one eye? That's great. Go get it." Crazed laughter, "Should I?" "Absolutely. Go do it." "Ok." She nods decisively. "I will." "Goodluck. You get em girl," I say. She disappears into the crowd, snaking towards the outback cyclops.

When I find Kial and Katie they look at me aporetically. "Yeah, I dunno. That chick is fuckin weird. She's up to something. Harry Potter bullshit." Katie smiles, I try and read it. Did she see me kissing her? No. Would she care if I did? No. Maybe? No. I can't tell. She might be good at pretending, but she's not being clear. There was as though an invisible glass between us. Bi? Is Katie picking up on that? Fuck, she thinks I'm gay? Surely not. I think I've made my interest clear without it being weird. Either way, it doesn't matter. Whatever. Katie starts dancing with a tall cowboy in a Northface jacket. She looks to me as though to ask 'is this fine?' But so subtly I can't tell whether I'm imagining it. To make it clear it's fine I'm clapping for her as he spins her around to these country classics that they both seem to know so well. Possession is not my thing. They're pulling moves and twists and heel kicks and dust is flying around and they're enjoying it in unison and I'm clapping for them and laughing. I'm encouraging it, why not? She doesn't belong to me. I just made out with a beautiful idiot over there. So, whatever. The tall Northface cowboy leans in and slips words into Katie's ear numerous times throughout their dance. After they've been at it for two songs or so she starts to pull away and shake her head after he leans in to her. She smiles condescendingly and keeps dancing country dances with him, her long orange skirt twirling in the stomping breeze. She likes me. But she's giving me and gave me nothing of that romantic aroma that wafts around the eyeballs like a red mist, love, love, love. There was no love. I move back and catch a glance of the Harry Potter idiot and she shoots a smile my way like a fuckin bullet. She's hot. Yep, definitely hot. Blonde and bodied well. What's her obsession with me? I shoot one back. She comes over and grabs me under the upper arm, tightly, leans against me with the whole of her body, "HEY!" "Hey, did you make out with one eye over there?" "No. he didn't want to." "Oh, what? That's no fun." "I know! Hey, I gotta pee, will you come with me?" "Ummm... yeah I guess. Why don't you ask your boyfriend though?" "No, I want you to come with me." "What are you doing?" "Nothing!" she exclaims. I look at Katie, Kial is looking around for things to shoot in the darkness of flickering stage lights. "Ok," I say. She grabs my hand and pulls me down the race track in the opposite direction that Kial and the Bronco Buster went last night. We go through all the lights. The lights from the canteen bar. Everyone can see me and her. And everyone can see her holding my hand. She's practically dragging me, "Ok, ok." We get down the dust track where it becomes less lit and she pulls herself to me and I abide and pull her in closer. "What are you doing? You're playing a game with him, aren't you?" "No, I'm not!!" She bursts with chaotic laughter like a geyser. It's unsettling. She's laughing like a maniac. Little witch. She pulls herself away from me but keeps holding my hand. She rolls herself back into me and looks at me again. She wants more. I lean in. She leans up. We kiss a dry and dusty fucking desert kiss. It's not satisfying. It's barely nice. It's stiff and arid. Entirely nothing. She can't even kiss anyway, she can't kiss good. And she pulls away again and that psychotic laughter emanates, echoes around the track. "You're fucking crazy," I tell her sincerely. She laughs again. Cackles. "Seriously though. I know you're doing something. You're poisonous, you silly thing." She twirls around in the dirt. Her cackle is now a giggle. She looks me in the eye and lets out another big laugh. "Hold my hand when I'm peeing!" she demands. "Ok, ok. Fucking, if he sees me… I'm not getting into a fight because of you, you realise, you're not worth it." "HA!" She's squatting by the side of the track in the dark, I can see a stream of piss running out of her. Her knees are touching. I wanna see where it's coming from. I wish I could see. But she's not flashing and I'm not kneeling over to take a look. As she pisses into the dirt she asks, "So, you're bi?" "Yeah, well, look, I'm straighter than I am gay, put it that way." "What! No way! I thought it was the other way around!" she exclaims and starts pulling up her jeans. "No, no. Why? Why would you think that?" Her face has changed. She's feeling self-conscious. "I just thought you were definitely more gay." I laugh. And she ducks under the barricade and walks next to me. "No, no." I reiterate. "What are you doing with this kid? C'mon? I see what you're doing, making him jealous. Why're you doing this?" "I'm not!" She laughs again maniacally and spins herself around and falls into my arms as we walk. "Yes, you are. You're crazy and you're trouble." I tell her and she says, "Kiss me again." So, I do. And it's just as shit and dry as the last one and she skips down the track holding my hand, gleeful as a little bee and when we get to the crowd I see her cowboy shoot a glance at her. She turns her back to him and looks at me lit up like electricity. I've never seen so many blue eyes. So, so blue. I shake my head and let go of her hand and move back to Kial standing near the fence, watching the dancing unfold, holding his camera, cycling through photos.

The Northface cowboy has left and I'm chatting to Kial and suddenly a song comes on, the same song as every other country song that has been played as far as I'm concerned and all these guys are taking off their pants. Denim is pulled down left right and center and guys are trotting around in their underwear and we see Katie clapping and laughing so we merge with her and I ask what the fuck is going on. "You don't know this? Every time this song plays all the blokes take down their pants and dance in their undies!" "Are you fuckin serious?" asks

Kial. "Yeah!" she exclaims. "What the fuck dude?" I say to Kial. "I dunno. This is pretty weird," he says. And he starts shooting pictures of guys in their undies. And a group start dancing around Katie and she's clapping and trotting or whatever you wanna call it, doing a jig or some shit and she points at one of em and says, "Get em off big boy! Go on." And he cranes his neck to the side feigning apprehension and says, "Erggh, fuck, alright." He undoes his belt and lets his jeans drop to his ankles around his cowboy boots and he starts trotting around in the dust and Katie's laughing and I'm laughing and Kial's laughing. "You go on!" says the guy to me, stomping around stupidly in his underwear. "Nah man." "Nah, fucking you go on!" he yells, his lips skewed with drunkenness, his hair all fucked, white sunnies hanging off his t-shirt collar. "Nah fuck off. I'm not doing that, man." And he turns away and disappears into the giant fish neat of cowboy hats. Men with either undone pant buckles or undoing pant buckles are all shuffling to this dumb country song that I wish so badly I could remember now, but I can't, and I can't because it sounded the fucking same as the rest of them. Katie leans in and says, "See this kid, Big Dick Energy!" I look at the guy. He's about 6"4, cowboy hat, what's new? Stripy blue shirt, dark blue denim, cowboy boots, lean and handsome. He looks about 22, but he's strolling around, pants down like he owns the shit.

Like it's his camel race. "Yeah, no shit," I shout back to her. "Good for him." "Yeah, he's into it! Why don't you get into it?" "Into what?" "Let loose. Don't be so uptight." "I'm not uptight, I'm just not taking my pants down to dance to this song." "Oh, c'mon!" she says, "Both of you." Kial looks at me and simply shakes his head. "No chance Katie. No chance." "You guys!" she says, disappointed and keeps dancing to whatever the fuck is playing. This stupid live fucking band. Old blokes. Beards. Twangin,' twigging, whatever. Shit.

After the song they play some other garbage and Katie leans in and says, "What about this song? This is great, look at him go, the guitarist!" I lean back and say, "Guitar solos can get fucked. They're so phallic." "Phallic!" she shouts, laughing. "Yeah, phallic." "Oh, well, I'll have to remember that. That's good!" She hasn't realised guitar solos are phallic? How? How in the hell. Oh, that's right, she likes contemporary country music. "Look, I'll teach ya how to barn dance birthday boy." "Alright, great. Let's do it." She's surprised. I hand Kial my drink and he chuckles. Katie starts by making me twirl her around, in and out a few times. Then she counts, 1, 2, 3, 4, 5, 6, 7 and we walk side by side forwards, then backwards the same, then we turn and touch boot soles. Then I twirl her twice and we do the same thing again, linking arms, 1, 2, 3, 4,

5, 6, 7 turn relink arms and walk forward. "You've never done this before?" she asks. "No, never. I had a deb once, that's it." "We learned this at school. We would have barn dances every few weeks and we had to learn all the dances." "For school?" "Yeah! for school! That's how we met people." "Right, right." "I'm a country girl. This is what it was like. It was the best." So, she's not from Thornbury? I swear last night she said she was from Thornbury at some point. I guess she just lived there a while. Where'd she grow up? Well, it's too late to ask her now. All I know is that she's definitely country and she's teaching me barn dances. She teaches me a few more and I get em wrong and we laugh and I fall against her shoulder and laugh at myself, and that's the movest move I've made so far and she laughs and says, "It's ok. Maybe we stop? You should learn to dance though. How have you never learned to dance?" "What barn dance? Haha, there's no reason for me to barn dance in Melbourne." "Well, how about you make me a promise? I know a place in Thornbury that teaches salsa, you get lessons. It'll give you life!" "I've wanted to learn to salsa for a while now actually, so, you know what, I can make that promise." We shake on it. "Fuck, I have such bitch hands, right? They're so soft." She strokes my hands and laughs, "Yeah, wow, you've never done a hard day's work in yer life!" "I actually used to be a furniture removalist." She nods disbelievingly. "No, really. Me, look at me. So stupid. It was the worst." She just nods and laughs and still doesn't believe me. "Wanna grab another drink?" I ask. "Yep," she answers. "Kial! Drink?" I yell to him behind his camera. He looks over and says, "Yip." We all three go and line up at the canteen. Kial and her talk and I piss in the cement toilets and just look around thinking. Thinking about barn dances and how weird whatever this is, is.

When we come away from the bar thing Kial and Katie are in front of me and the church girl from the hill is talking to Katie. I walk up. "Hey!" she yells with that meme face, you know the one of the obsessive girlfriend, well that's her face, but blonde and she's better looking. "Heya." "How you doing?!" "Yeah, good." "Having fun?!" "Yeah, it's fine." "Haha!" I turn to Katie, "Let's go back down." She looks at me confused. "Anyway, I'll see you round," I say to church girl. "Ok!" she says. Katie, Kial and I descend to the pit. "What was that about?" asks Katie. "Sorry, just needed to get away from that girl." "Why?" "Ah, she was talking to us today, and she just seems crazy. I dunno. Too much. Too into me. Was freaking me out." Katie laughs with confusion and says, "Ok." And we dance some more down there, but mostly Kial and I watch and sit back and it gets late and I say to Katie, "Hey, did you still wanna sit around that fire? Our camp neighbours have one and they said we could use it whenever we wanted." Which was true. As lookalike as these folks were, our neighbours were nice, as I'm sure everyone kinda was, but within a certain framework. "Do you have snacks?" she asks. I turn to Kial, "Yeah we have snacks," Kial says. "We have some hummus." "We gotta bit of celery, carrots. Yeah, I dunno. Maybe some corn chips." "What have you boys been eating?" "We don't really eat that much." Kial says. "Foods not really a thing," he adds. "What?" "Yeah, we didn't bring much, but we're fine." I say. "Ok, well, if there's snacks I'll come back and you can read me your ending." "Yeah! that's right. I can." "Wanna go?" I ask Kial. Yeah, fuck it. Let's go." We walk back, through the gate, past the food trucks and stalls that have mostly closed, past the somnolent carnie rides, the cold air whistling, past the bin where we dump our Emus on the way in, down the dust road and back to site. And Katie says to me, "My friend says, just don't go back to a campsite with someone called Sloan. That's the only warning she gave me when I spoke to her the other day. She just said, promise me that. So, this is funny." "Oh, shit… What are the chances of it being a Sloan too? Jesus. Well, fuck, I dunno how to feel now? This is weird. It's just up there… umm… look, if you don't wanna come back, that's totally cool. Seriously." "No, no, it's just really funny." Yeah, real funny. I feel like a creep. It's tainted. What am I doing? "I'm just gonna message my friend because it's so funny." "Yeah, please do that wouldn't you." And as we walked I kept pointing out land marks for her so she knew where she was and she laughed it off and said it was fine and it was funny. We got to camp and I showed her our car with some sort of pride in its simplicity, our tent again with the same simplicity and pride, and she just nodded. We opened the boot and sat on the edge of it and dipped corn chips and celery into hummus. "Sorry, there's less than I thought," I say. "It's ok," She assures and takes a big dollop with a corn chip. "Let's sit by the fire," I said. I grabbed the hummus tub, "You want a beer?" I ask. "Ummm…" "You wanna share one?" Kial asks. "Yeah, I'll share one." I grab one for myself, give one to Kial, and one to her and tell her we'll help her share hers. Cross legged we all sit by the embers of our neighbours fire and we look at the stars and she says, "So, are you gonna read your ending or what?" "Yeah, yeah, sorry. A bit nervous. You all ready?" "Yep." "Yeah." "Ok, ahem. There are strange moments of vulgarity – an ethos of unknowing. What you don't feel won't hurt you. And maybe there is a truth in that. But it's still fucked cause it isn't truth that dictates our lives, it's what you feel, it's what you channel. It's your narrative and how it merges with others. This is Channel Country, where nobody takes responsibility for who they are, who they affect, or anything, nearly anything that even happens.

And I write this drinking on one knee by a children's carnie ride as that red hot sun sinks once again, and I'll never get used to seeing it sink like this. But I know, everywhere on earth, it's sinking, just different…."

There's a silence. Kial lets out a "Mmm," swallowing it up through his nerves. And Katie says, "I like the start, the vulgarity is true." "Should I read it again?" "Yeah, yeah, read that again. It's getting better every time I hear it," says Kial. "Ok, ok, ahem. There are strange moments of vulgarity – an ethos of unknowing. What you don't feel won't hurt you. And maybe there is a truth in that. But it's still fucked cause it isn't truth that dictates our lives. It's what you feel, it's what you channel. It's your narrative and how it merges with others. This is Channel Country, where nobody takes responsibility for who they are, who they affect, or anything, nearly anything that even happens.

And I write this drinking on one knee by a children's carnie ride as that red hot sun sinks once again, and I'll never get used to seeing it sink like this. But I know, everywhere on earth, it's sinking, just different."

"Yep. It's good," says Kial. "Yeah. I like it," says Katie and in her agreeableness, I feel her float away from me, or me from her, or maybe we never floated together really at all.

"How can you know it's the end before it's even finished?" she asks. "Well, I mean, I don't know for sure. But it feels like it's right. I can't explain it. I don't know what will happen. But I feel like it, ummm…" and I make a scooping shape with my arm, like rounding something out, the size of myself, from thin air. "I feel like it does this, I feel like it'll do this, ya know? I mean it seems stupid, but like this," and I make the shape again. "No, I think I understand." I get the feeling she doesn't. We look up silently for a moment. "We should see a shooting star now," says Kial. And Katie and I agreed. And then one shoots past. "Holy shit." "What!" screams Katie, and she claps. And Kial goes, "Pffttt. Fuck," and then says, "Ok, well we should all have one each." So, we keep looking. "That one was yours," I tell him "Yeah, it was," he says. "Next one is yours," I tell Katie. And then whoosh! In silent space, another fucking shooting star. And we roar again in disbelief, but also somehow in total assurance. "Well, mine's next." And fuckin-whoosh. Again. "Jesus!" And then another and we slap our thighs and we drink our Emus and I smoke a cigarette a damn good cigarette. And we talk. And we are all evenly, triangularly apart. She is not near me. She is not near Kial. I am not near Kial. Kial is not near me. And the spectacle is just a thing. "Well, it's late. I should go. But let me cook you both breakfast tomorrow. You can't not eat the whole time." "No, it's fine," I say. "We're good," adds

Kial. "No, really. If you want to, let's have breakfast. I can bring it to you or you can come to me, I'm just over there." She stands up, brushes her tanned tall legs off and points to the distance, to nothingness and says, "I'm just there." She points, "I'll cook you a big breakfast tomorrow." "Ok. That'd be lovely," I say. "Ok," agrees Kial. "Well, I should head back now." "Where are you? I can walk you if you like?" "No, you don't have to do that." "Nah, it's fine. I'd like to know you get back safely." "I drove to the gate. It's ok. You don't have to." "Nah, I will. It's all good. That's not far." "Ok," she says then says goodbye to Kial. And I say, "I'll be back soon," to him and I walk her down the dirt road towards the gate. And we talk about breakfast and I tell her how nice it's been meeting her and she says the same. She points out her car when we get near. It's a big Toyota thing, dark silver like the police car that pulled us over. "So, you're good to drive back?" "Yeah, been doing it every night. Right as rain. You want a lift back?" "Nah, nah, it's fine. I'll walk. I just wanted to make sure you got back alright." "You sure you don't want a lift?" "Yeah, really, it's ok. I'll walk." I say in some defeat, in realisation. This isn't taking that course. How much did I want it to? Maybe I wanted to go the full way into her, through her barriers, to be alone in her. Intimacy would have revealed something that she didn't want to reveal in conversation for whatever reason. Maybe I just didn't know what I was doing anymore. Or maybe I'm taking about myself here. It's been so long. And non-monogamy is new and a little terrifying. But I was sure she liked me. I didn't know what was happening. But it was over. She didn't want me that way. And that's ok. Would I have wanted her that way? I mean, yeah, absolutely. And I started on walking back down the dirt track, and she drove past, and I waved and she waved and drove off down another track and I thought of that young hot thing with the dusty mouth and the poor boy that was only just learning about girls like that. And I thought about the crazed church girl from Mt Isa and how I could have fucked her and how it would have been good. Maybe? Would it have been? No. No, this was right. This emptiness was right. This misreading of everything was right for whatever reason. It was all right. In its place. Its displaced place. Birthday. And when I got back to camp I poked my head in Kial's tent. "Kial?" "Hey! You're back? What happened?" "Nothing. Nothing at all. Nothing was there. Nothing at all." I cracked an Emu, and I sat against the boot and I rolled a cigarette and I smoked it and I looked down at the earth and I looked up at the sky. I crawled into my tent and crawled into my sleeping bag, and I felt the cold soft dirt through the floor, and Kial and I talked through our tents about who knows what for just a little while before falling asleep at a different age.

5

Whatever, Whatever, Whatever

I awoke drunk. I heard Kial get up and roll around a bit a few times, but I must have fallen asleep again, which was the aim. I then awoke to Kial outside the tent pouring water or squeezing water from a 4-liter receptacle that didn't work. The latch button thing didn't work. We'd stabbed a large hole into the top to get the air in, to force the water out, but nothing was working for us. Anyway, he was squeezing that water into a bottle, a more manageable receptacle and I felt the heat of the tent. A small sauna. A good repose from the chilling wake-up that occurred throughout the night. I would wrap my head up in the sleeping bag if it got too cold, which it did, then I'd unwrap it when it got too hot and I'd repeat that throughout. But it was still a better sleep than last night, and distinctly better than two nights prior. There were no horrendously prolific dreams. There was no agony. I just went to bed on my birthday at an age I'd never gone to bed before. Kial was, as usual, up before me. "What's going on with the breakfast thing?" I asked. "Umm... I dunno. She drove past before and asked if we wanted breakfast still, and I said 'sure' and then she drove off." "Ok, fuck. I can't be fucked going for breakfast. Is she bringing it here?" I yelled from the tent. "I dunno. She just asked if we wanted it. I dunno if she's bringing it or if we have to go find her." "Fuuucckkkkk…" I squirmed uncomfortably in the sack. I could feel a stone or something under me. Fucking shit. "I think I'm still drunk!" I called. "Mmm…" said Kial in agreeance or out of carelessness. I couldn't tell. Didn't care. I could hear him sipping water. "I was gonna say, we go into town, get some fresh beers for today. You know, a six pack of something cold. This ice is melting. The Emus are getting warm. But, I don't wanna drive. I feel like that speeding ticket was a sign. So, I don't want to drive. You can't drive?" he added. "Nah, man, I skulled that emu out of sexual frustration last night at whatever time and I'm still drunk maybe. I mean… I could drive…. But nah. Nah, I shouldn't drive." "Feck" said Kial. "Maybe she could drive us into town?" He proposed. Must've been still drunk too. "Yeah, maybe." I said. "I mean. I dunno. Probably. So, what do we do? We have to wait around here for her or something? Or do we go find her?" I emerged from the tent, disheveled, dry mouthed. Kial handed me some water. I drank it. "I dunno. She just drove up, asked if we wanted breakfast then drove off when I said 'sure'." "So, she's definitely making us breakfast?" I asked with a mouthful of wet wet water, the wettest fuckin water. "I dunno," said Kial. "Fuck," I said. I leaned on the white boot of the car. Took in the hot sun. It was so fucking hot. I knew today I'd wear my small yellow shorts all day. Fuck it. Get these pale puppies some tan. I slid on my chucks from the front seat. Returned to the boot to lean and drink water. "Well, I need coffee man," I said. "Yeah, me too." "So, is she coming back or what? I need to get coffee or something. I'm hungry too, maybe the breakfast is actually a great idea. I just wish I knew if she was bringing it back here or if she expects us to know where she's camped from that vague direction she pointed at last night?" "Yeah, I dunno. She just asked if we wanted breakfast, I said 'sure' then she drove off," said Kial again. "Fuck. I guess I'll just read or whatever. And we'll wait a few hours? FEW HOURS? Fuckin hell. Anyway, I guess we wait? She's nice. And a hot meal sounds good. A cooked meal with vegetables sounds nice. I guess we wait around for a while then just fuck off at some point?" "Yeah, I guess." "But, man, I really need coffee." "Ergh, ok, well, I should go get it?" "Nah. I wanna get it," I said. "Yeah, but if she comes back, you should be the one who talks to her." "Erhg, fuck. Ok. Fine. I don't wanna just sit around the fucking car all morning though." "Yeah. Me either. But this is more your problem." "Yeah, you're right. Ok." I pulled Exley out and flicked through the pages. "Ok. Well, yeah. I guess, a double espresso." I say. "Or long black?" asks Kial.

"Hmm… nah, double espresso." "Ok, cool," he says angling the borrowed camera comfortably round his shoulder, "I'll be back soon." "Alright. Ciao." "Ciao." He walked off and I sat down under the tree where the ants bit his ass and I read and I drank water and I rolled a cigarette and I smoked it and I looked out for Katie and she didn't come. Then I sat in the front seat of the car and read with my feet resting on the top of the car door and kept an eye out for Katie, and it was no good. It had been an hour or so until Kial returned. "They're out of coffee." "What? Are you fucking kidding me?" He laughed, "No, seriously, they're all out of coffee." "What the fuck!? Erghhh. So, now we wait here all morning and do nothing and not even coffee?" I feel like killing myself. "I dunno," said Kial. "Maybe Katie has some?" he says. "Yeah, maybe. She did say she had some." "Yeah, well. Should we go find her?" "Yeah, fuck, I guess. Fuck! Ok, whatever." I kept on the tiny yellow shorts, had a white t-shirt and linen shirt over the top and white chucks, low at the ankle. And Kial wore his denim jeans, white cut off T and boots, how I admired those boots he had. They made him tall, lean, angry. And I had Paladiums, fucking Star Wars boots. Or chucks. At least I had them. But they made me feel short. Like a bitch. Like a little bitch amongst these cowboys and against Katie. She was my height in her cowboy boots. That was ok. But I didn't feel strong. And shoes have a lot to do with that. They always do. And Kial felt strong or at least he looked it, and I felt meek like a little perforated bag of dried lavender. "Let's go find her fucking van shit thing then, whatever," I coughed. "She said she was near the creek." Said Kial. "The creek? What? There's a creek?" "Yeah, she said over there." "Cool. I didn't hear that. Whatever." "Yeah, well, I dunno." "Ok." I coughed again. Then I coughed a lot. We walked over towards where she listlessly pointed and apparently mentioned there was a creek. "She asked me for my number, so I gave it to her and I said that I didn't have any reception, like, four times, and she still wanted my number," Kial said. "What? But what is she gonna do with your number when you have no reception?" "Exactly. So, I gave her my number and she gave me hers and said call me even though I said I don't have reception and she said, 'well I'll call you.' What an idiot." "What the fuck? That makes no sense. What an idiot." "Yeah I know. She couldn't understand that she couldn't call me when I have no reception. I dunno. Or she didn't believe me, or she just wanted something tangible." "Yeah, fuck. Well, this sucks." "Yeah, well, let's just walk towards where she said the creek was?" So, we did. And we found a creek. And it was big, it was wide. Nearly a river. I suppose out here it's a creek, but at home it's a river.

We walked through the scattered caravan set-ups along the bank and found nothing resembling the car that she'd climbed into when I'd walked her back to the gate last night. We walked for an hour maybe, and nothing. "Let's just go back to the tent. This is useless." The sun was becoming unbearable. "Yeah, it's getting late, we should go check out what races they have on today and when they start," said Kial. "Yeah, fuck this. So, when she came by… did she give some kind of hint as to whether she would be waiting for us for breakfast or whether she'd bring it to us?" "No, I couldn't tell. She just asked if we still wanted breakfast…" "Yeah, yeah, yeah. Ok, ok. Goddamn it." We walked back and the sun was getting raw on us. My shorts were up high and I could feel my pale thighs sizzling. We got back to the car and lathered ourselves in sunscreen. I felt like coffee. Kial felt like coffee. This was no good. We got ourselves prepared. I kept looking out for Katie on the road. But it was no good. We drank an Emu quick and got stressed about our vanishing alcohol and lack of ice. Katie could drive us in if we found her maybe? Maybe she just went home though? Who knows with anybody. Frustration was on me like a little yappy dog, a snake lunch barking at the door. I was annoyed. Horny. Hungry. She may have fulfilled all these voids. But, whatever, that's all I could keep thinking when I heard the little piercing fuckin' yap of dissatisfaction. It's the only respite. It's the only thing that quells self-inflicted annoyance- "Whatever, whatever, whatever." We walked down the dusty path to whatever.

✶
Camel Tagging

The canteen was desolate. A few people around, barely. Meaty cheese food places were still open, but nobody was really lining up. Drink cards were still being slung, so we grabbed a few. I needed food, so I figured sugar was a reasonable substitute. Plus, I needed caffeine, so grout cleaner tasting Bundy and coke it was. I got four spirit tickets and four beer tickets. They wouldn't last long. Not today, not usually, but not today. It was clear where everyone was now as we walked down the embankment. There were the industrial sized fishing nets of cowboy hats bobbing along the fence line of the camel pen. Bootcut jeaned legs clambering over rusted steel poles, children hugging at parent's knees, Oakley sunglasses, double-chins, sequin embroidery, XXXX cans, hollering and shouting, yee-hawing, thigh slapping. People were clustered together all around. A microphone pierced through the dumb fodder of yells and claps. "Ladies and gentleman, if you'd like to give it a crack, please line up now to the left of the gate. Now, these young camels are wild camels, so they've got a lot of kick in em. They're feisty buggers." A man in his early twenties takes off his cowdee hat and hands it to the fat thing manning the gate to the pen. He enters. The red ground is soft dirt. This has some sour waft of a bullfight but without any grace. And yes, there is grace in a bullfight despite its insidiousness. There are three camels in cages, like you'd see bulls. It's the same sort of deal. Some dipshit lifts the gate lock and swings it open when the speaker crackles, "GO!" The camels bursts out, meanders out, cowers out, hops out, lurches out, depending on its disposition. The asshole who's giving this tagging 'a crack' has blue sticky tape flapping from his hand. He eagerly awaits the opening of the camel pen. The camel inside is circling itself inside the cage like a domesticated dog before sitting down somewhere half-comfortable, but it's got nowhere to sit. It's scared shitless. The thing is terrified. Thick goop in the long lashes of its perpetually teary eyes, it backs away from the gate. "Alright, you ready there, mate?!" The asshole waves to the crowd and the crowd cheers and roars and all that nonsense you'd expect. "Get em, Micky!" yells a woman edging in next to me at the fence. "Sorry love, that's my friend in there," she says apologising for the hissing shout she cracked in my ear. "S'all good," I say, "enjoy yourself." She smiles. Her teeth don't match the sparkling rhinestones on the front pockets of her black studded shirt. Instead, her teeth are more aligned with her leather Akubra that's sucking on her head, greenish and worn down. Her ass is a melon like the rest. Her boots are cowboy boots. Ranch boots. Cattle boots. I sip my beer. "3, 2, 1, Get em!" The gate is opened, the camel lowers its head, then dips it to the side and up like a boxer, instinctively for self-preservation. Asshole Micky has his hands spread out wide to make himself more intimidating. The camel stomps its front hooves into the dust, bucking. "Get em, Micky!" I hear again. Micky runs up to the young wild camel and it sprints away from him. He dodges back off the ball of his cowboy booted left foot and the camel turns and gallops back. Micky slows. The camel backs itself into the furthest fence from him. I can see into its yolky fearful eyeball. Micky fakies to his left and the camel falls for it. Coming back to his right he gets the blue tape on the shoulder of the thing just as it kicks out its helicoptering leg. The fatal hooved flick misses Micky. The crowd goes, "Ooooooo!" Next to me there's a shrill screech, "WOOHOO! That's it, Mick!" I sip my beer. Over the microphone, "That's it. That's it. Now touch the fence! Don't forget to touch the fence." Micky runs to the fence next to the gate where he entered and slaps the pole. The camel turns around so that the shoulder with the tape is no longer facing him. "Oh, you gotta get him around. That's it. That's it!" the announcer spits. Micky does a fakie again, the camel isn't fooled. He runs up behind it waving his arms in the air. The camel turns and faces away from him and he runs towards its shoulder, it takes off and gets to the other side of the pen now and Micky does another fakie, but the camel's shoulder with the tape is again facing away from him. He has to get the tape back. Mick is shouting something at the wild thing, its legs swing out almost snapping Mickie's shins and the crowd goes, "Ooooooo," and some guys in the back go, "Yeah. Fuckin' get him!" And they're cackling depraved cowdee cackles.

Kial strolls around the corner with the certain confidence of a paid journalist. His gait. He'd been snapping photos of the camels in their pens. Their hapless terror was indignant. And everyone overlooked it. There was fun to be had after all in traumatizing the youth out of wild adolescence, right? We took two oxazepam each because we didn't know what else to do. It was clear everything was being knotted up after the camel tagging. People dispersed and dumped cups into bins and retreated into the far corners of the hot sun that stretched itself across the track and the dying grass and the rusted rides and the crappy food trucks and the concrete canteen. The oxazepam added to the junkyard feeling in us as we walked around the empty chairs and tables near the tracks. The midday heat was burning bright and we didn't want to sit in the canteen with all the cowdees, so we opted to go back to the car and pull open the few warm Emus we still had.

**
Eggs And Cum

We were aimless back at camp. The neighbour's fire smoldered in the shade of a gum. We got in the car and drank and considered a drive to the bottle shop in town but it wasn't worth the risk. By every indication the races weren't happening today. Yesterday must've been the final and we missed it. How did we manage to fuck this up? We grazed on time until we'd had our fill of slouching and car-seat drinking and talking. Kicking the dust like a tin can we returned slightly more drunk, but much more relaxed to the racing area where there were no more races. We caught sight of Katie with her friend and her friend's two kids playing in the dirt by the side of the track. She had a drink in her hand and was moving around like she'd had a few. "Hey boys! What happened to breakfast, ey?" she piped, not without reservation. "Katie, we were looking everywhere for you. We walked up and down where you pointed last night but we couldn't find your site anywhere." I said. "Yeah, sure," she winked. What the hell was this? We should be pissed at her. We'd waited all morning. We'd done nothing all day in lieu of this fucking promised breakfast. "Well, no skin off my teeth. More for me. I've got dinner tonight." She quipped. I sighed, "Damn it. Sorry." Why was I apologising? Fucksake. I continued,

"We were looking forward to it all morning." "It's true," said Kial innocently. "What'd you make anyway?" I asked. "Well, I cooked up some eggplant, chickpeas, loads of veg. I went into town this morning to buy it all." "Oh, shit, seriously?" "Yeah, but it's fine." It obviously wasn't totally fine. But it was what it was. "You want a drink?" I asked. "Nah, got one. Tam, this is Sloan and Kial, the boys who missed out on breakfast." "Ah, yep. Sounds like you boys sure did miss out." "Yeah, it does, doesn't it?" We cashed our drink cards in and returned to the girls. "The camel tagging was pretty wild wasn't it!? Jesus! Those things can kick. I was going to go do it, ya know. I was meant to be in last, but I just missed out. They said the last one was right before me!" "Oh, yeah? Hmm... I would've liked seeing you in there waving around a piece of blue tape, I think." She added, "I did feel bad for the camels sometimes though. Looked a bit rough on the poor things." She lied. She thought of what I would think instead of how she felt and she thought of how she would be judged. A circle is now forming around the other entrance to this grassy side embankment and a fat fella struts around with a mic. "Testing 1, 2, 1, 2. Yep, mate we got it." Thumbs up from him. "Alright ladies and gents, we got another fierce event starting. The one you've all been waiting for. That's right folks, the yabby racing is just about to start." What on earth is going on? "Yeah, that's right they have a yabby race, fucking hell," says Kial. "What the fuck?" "Gotta get this. I think, anyway. I dunno." "Yeah, I mean. I guess it's something." "Might actually be better than the camel racing." "This is true." The mic-wielding fatty looks like a Shell servo pie. He quacks on about the size of the yabbies as the recognizable tall fella with a clean cowboy hat (Big Dick Energy) takes the yabbies out of a bucket and holds them up to the sun so the small crowd gathering around a square of foam rubber can see them and place their bets. Big Dick Energy pulls one out, about 2 inches long, not so chunky. "How much we got for this fella?! Could be quick, speedy, could let loose on the turf. Do we have $20? $20? Anyone, $20?" "Yeah, I'll go $50 on him!" shouts a swollen faced flannelette. "$50 ladies and gents. $50! Can we get $60?" "Yeah, $60 over here!" The crowd circling around laughs. Kids duck in through the standing audience, they set up chairs and climb onto them for a better view. The crowd is thickening up so much that I climb onto a chair myself and Kial weaves through the lewd bastards to snap away at the spectacle. The second yabby is plucked outta a bucket and Big Dick Energy holds him up to the sunlight. Servo pie yaks on about prices and the bets are placed, some absurd amount, and then the two yabbies are put together in the middle of the mat. There's a circle drawn around the center where the two yabbies are that acts as the finish line. The bucket is lifted and the first yabby to cross the edge of the circle wins. Kids are kneeling down with spray bottles, squirting the yabbies to entice them to move their pathetic crawlin' legs. They wobble and pinch and turn on their back as the crowd start hollering and shouting and yee-hawing. What on earth is going on? Are my eyes rolling back in my head? I can't grasp this shit. One of the yabbies wins and the other loses. Wow, right? They both go back in a bucket somewhere and the next two yabbies are plucked out and held up to the sun for bet placing. "$130!" yells a voice. What is this? Where's all this money coming from? What'd they bet on the camels? "$250!" I take off my sunglasses. "$290!" The crowd laugh and cheer. "$300!" The bucket comes off the two in the center and they scramble and the kids on their knees at the edges of the makeshift track squirt and spray and squirt the hot dark shells of the ambling critters. The bucket is filled with them. Hard exteriors and pincers. Beady fucking eyes. They're stuck. Trapped. Can they grasp crossing a finish line? Can they comprehend success? But their win isn't success anyway. Only for the sea of hats that ebb and flow violently around them, waving fistfuls of bright plastic money, barking and hooting, only for them is there any contrived success. I move off into the shade to light a cigarette and write:

The tiny crowd is the reality. The nonsense. The prices

paid. The gambling under hot sun. These people are the truth here. The others came to party and barn dance, to kick in the camel track dust. And the booze runs out and out, over and over. Kids wearing fingerless gloves for yabby protection. People standing on chairs. Screaming into mics and for what? Now whittled down to fifty people. The excitement is both real and fake. They're creating their own. Their groupthink. Group-hype. It's not human connection. It's behind it. It's what is in the human reciprocation when it's drowsy and languid. When it's dissipating. You're faced with your convictions. Head-fucking on. Shit is shit. You can tell by the smell. And whether you enjoy it or not, it's still fecal, it's still shit. It still fucking stinks. Not that I didn't know. Not that it wasn't already painfully obvious, but kindness isn't worth a thing when it's segregated, when it's an event. When it's only through recognition of the self or some other kind of emotion - as a fist drawn back. Rationality takes precedence. Relations are vapid. We need more. There's fragile hedonistic backward humanity here. Real white humanity. Grotesque reality is hard to face. The stomach is rancid. And if we weren't drinking, I simply couldn't cope with it. Hell is found in other people. The final yabby event reaches $2600 to take home.

I stay in the shade, smoking, sipping my cup of laundry

liquid Bundy and watching some of the hell finish up, pack up, and move on. And I write about reflections of country music and Katie. The music is safe and familiar. So, it makes sense that these folks are into it. It doesn't test any boundaries. You know what it's about and where it's gonna go. Black is black and white is white and yabby is yabby. But to me it's not. It never is. A yabby is never just a yabby. The Min Min lights aren't just the Min Min lights. They aren't what they are on the brochure. They're a whole bunch of shit. And some of that is special if you want it to be. But most of it isn't. Unless you have a story to attach to these gassy deposits which I doubt we'll see, then you have nothing special at all to take from them. The shooting stars, now that was something. And the fireworks, well they were really something too. But only something to me, just like the camel races are really something to these people. I've come here for something like everyone else. I've come here to see whatever this thing is. And it's stupid. That's what I've ascertained. Is the best this story can be an exercise in futility? Like Katie's outback escape to dignify herself with purpose and meaning I thought the story would write itself. I would be its vessel. But it all falls short. Why the pressure? Why the dread? I'm grasping at straws throughout this whole event. Looking for a link in every experience. And what she really needs to look for is nothing. She found what was nothing in a full-time job, a nothingness of the self because it's all given away to unappreciative others, and now she has to find nothingness all over again out here, but for herself. I think that's the only way. And I'm seeing it everywhere. In every fat face. In every doe eyed girl. In every cattleman's gamblin' hand. In every overpriced drink and at the bottom of every little plastic cup. In every thing apart from looking out into the sunset at nothingness itself. There's nothingness and then there's absence and to be absent is far worse than it is to be nothing.

The meat pie with the mic sips his Bundy and cola and announces that the kids tug o' war is about to begin on the track. Kial and I meet and get a drink and shake our heads. Trying to place what is happening is consistently becoming more and more difficult. And I thought my birthday was confusing. I suppose we have to allow this attempt at a story and attempt at a photo series to be what it is with its mundane and impertinent value, we have to reveal it for what it is. An event. And so far, a failure. We decide to walk up past the kids knotting themselves in heavy rope and shoot those that were camel racers that are hanging out behind some trucks and caravans. We pass a couple of camels lying down in pens baking in the sun. I walk up to the steel beams and take a look. I look into the giant eyeball. A black shining pool of experience.

Why is it so easy to see the humanity in this long-lashed thing? This sad and worried young animal. I sink into its melancholia. It yearns for something else, something that's not a squalid square cage. It longs for something in its nature. You were once wild, I think. And now you only exist for others.

We walk into what feels like a tip-site. There's a fire pit, there's a few racers seated around drinking Johnnie Walker and cokes, mixing their own. They're eating Smiths chips. "Hey guys, I'm just shooting some photos of the event. You wouldn't mind if I got some photos of you with the jerseys, would you?" Kial asks. Perturbed, they look at each other, slumped in their fold out camp chairs. "Yeah, sorry, I see you're relaxing, won't take long though" Kial adds. "Nah, you're right, you're right," one bloke says begrudgingly. "You wouldn't mind, would you?" Kial persists. He has to, they're fucking sinking into whisky oblivion. This girl who looks like a BMX bandit stands up. "Alright, I'll do it mate." "Thanks so much. Appreciate it. Won't take long then you can get back to it." The blokey blokes nod. "You wanted the jersey? You want me to put it on?" She asks. "Nah, nah. You're right. Maybe just hold it up." She looks around a little confused and says shrugging, "Alright." "Ummm… where do I want you?" says Kial. We scope it out. The dump dive is pretty bleak. Kial wants the shimmering of the jersey, he has something coming together in his head. I can see it in him. He knows something that I don't quite understand yet, or maybe he's treading water on pure intuition. The camel racer stands against a trailer with her jersey held up. Another guy stands next to her and Kial snaps away. It's awkward. I don't bother making conversation with the chair slumped sloths. We thank them and leave and they get back to their drinking. Heading back to the track entrance we see people tugging at the giant rope like a twisted anaconda dead in the dirt. Servo Pie is quite drunk by the looks of things, stumbling around with the mic. People are taking off their shoes and stretching, getting ready for the next heat of tug o' war. We see Katie and her friend again and saddle up with them at the same spot by the fence.

They start with the kids, lil barely walkables tugging at the fat rope. Then they move to teens, then girls/women, this is when Katie runs in with her pal. Her friend says, "Do you mind watching my kids while I go do this?" Kial and l look at each other. Yeah, sure, we'll look after your kids… We're just two guys from interstate who have no idea who you are. Sure, sure. I watch her little blonde dweebs climb on the seats and smash trucks in the dirt near the fence and they start asking where mum is. I tell them she's tugging on a rope and point her out. They don't seem to comprehend. Which is reasonable because I don't either. I drink my tile cleaner and shake my head. "Look guys, she's just there. See her? That's ya mum! Wooo! Say, go mum!" I tell them. They look at me more perplexed. Yeah, I get it.

Katie and Co take the same end of the rope and get pulled into the dust by an impressive Heffalump leading the pull on the other end. They trudge back to us and I'm thanked for my babysitting. Well, I made sure the little fellas didn't die, I did alright. Katie opens up a bit and stops blaming us for the breakfast lapse, but I know it's not real. She holds a grudge. Strange. What about exactly? I sense it in her tone and her mannerisms. Maybe she did see me kiss that moron and I misread everything? Who's to know, but she's unable to hide an obvious tension. I wonder if grudges caused from simple mistakes have any relation to her escaping to the outback? Is she letting go of everything so she can hold onto something else? Are we? Am I? I mean, here we are attempting to give our lives some meaning through participating in an absurd event and creating what we can of it. Our perception carved out and unique. But of what? Being here is like artificial insemination. Now we are in gestation. What will the damn thing look like? We are confused and bloated with the eggs and cum of our future.

Katie and Co offer us a drink as thanks, "Sure," we say, course. Whilst they're gone we befriend a couple of fatty-ratties that are celebrating a weekend off from working at the cannery a few hours from here. One dude buttered with sunscreen, grimy-faced with a methy aura tells us his mum is coming later to visit and he's nervous cause he's been drunk for days. He can barely talk. He tangents about wanting to join the tug o' war. There's crazed sincerity behind his Oakley sunnies. Of course, I egg him on and so does his little pal. Egg, egg, egg. He yanks at the peak on his beanie and offers to buy us a drink and we say "Nah, it's all good," because we have drinks on the way, the girls are in line. And he says, "Nah nah, nah." And shuffles off. Then his mate gets up in my ear. Slur. Breath. "He's such a good guy, a cooked cunt, but mate. Such a-fuckin good bloke." "Yeah, yeah, I can see that man." "Yeah man. Ey, where you think I'm from?" "Umm… I dunno dude." "Yeah, well, fucking, all these cunts think I'm Mexican!" he giggles, high-pitched. "But I'm Filipino. You see that?" "Yeah, yeah, I do man. That makes sense." "Yeah, it's just like the mo, ey?" And he slides his grimy finger across his mo. "Yeah, probably." Anyway, we talk with these two weirdos for too long and drink free drinks off them which is nice. Katie and friend had long left for dinner or something after seeing us with these two messes. We watch and hang with our free drink buddies enjoying the free juice and getting some laughs amongst what has become and probably always was a strange dim circus. After the men had finished their tug o' war the two cannery clots invite us to their camp, they motion vague ass directions just like Katie's breakfast. But we say, "Yeah, yeah, yeah," and mean it because what else is happening? "Yeah, we'll definitely come hang guys. Looks like there's nothing else to do tonight." "Yeah, we got bottles of scotch, we got rum, coke, beers, guys, we love ya, don't we man?!" his mate says, elbowing the drunk methy Mumma's boy. "Fuckin too right! fuckin love you blokes." We didn't do anything deserving of their love but they had their arms around us. Seems fine. Free drinks. "Yeah, we'll come man." I say again and again. "We're just out the gate and by the big fire down the road on the corner. You can't miss it." "Right… so… we leave, then walk down that road on the left, then we'll just see you by the fire?" "Yeah." "Ok…" "If you can't find us, call out Cullum!! Ok?" "Yeah, alright." "Alright, we gotta head back," they say. So, we just stand around drunk watching the sun die. Fuck this shit. Fucking hell. I guess, we have no idea what is going on anymore. "We could shoot some UV pics?" I say. "Mmm… yeah maybe." Kial isn't sold on the idea so much anymore. "Or do we just get drunk with those guys?" "I dunno." "Yeah. Meh." I could find Katie? Nah. Nah. That ship has sailed. One thing to do. Make a half-assed promise and then head back to camp and reconvene. So, we do just that. Again. Car front seat. By now charging my phone doesn't mean anything. It always dies. It never worked out here anyway. I haven't heard from Fia or family for days. We sit in the dirt. It was my birthday. I don't care. Or do I? I don't care if I care. That's the thing. But I'm horny. That's real. Well, whatever. How horny am I? Katie wasn't putting down and I think I forgot how to pick up anyway. She didn't reciprocate concretely. That I know. I dunno what outback men do, but I await reciprocation. Or maybe I was meant to reciprocate? Whatever. Whatever. Whatever.

We smash the last of the Emus, there's maybe three or four left. We talk and we sit around. We grab our stuff and we rest and we talk into the real talk of the work and we get fucking nowhere again. It's all foggy. The only clarity here is in the perfect and empty sky, away from anything. Last night we figured something has to happen. Let's follow the stars, why the fuck not? And the stars say that those cannery rats from before seem like a fine idea. We got nothing better to do than sit by a bon fire with a pack of oddities and potentially take their stories, maybe their portraits, maybe that's not right. No, their portraits aren't right. But their stories, the evening tale... I dunno. We head back to the bar and get some dogwash for the walk back. "Should I get some ice for the eski? The

Emus are getting warm?" asks Kial. "Yeah, ask the bar for some ice." "Alright," Kial says. Then stops and looks at me, thinking. "Get them to fill up your hat with ice and we can carry it back," I say. Kial laughs, "Yeah, ok. See if that works." It does. So Kial and I walk back to the car with straw hat full of ice for our car-boot Emus. After a bout in the sedan we head off, beers in hand and one back-up stuffed into a pocket. There were more left than expected. We walk through the starlit dirt in search of promised bon fire. And we walk… and we walk… and we take the way past where we figure Katie is and Kial tells me to yell out her name so I do and people look up from their lantern-lit front verandas, from around their fires. They see two fools waltzing, two men, one long blonde and the other dirt browned, in trench coat, navy, faux fur collared. I walk and I yell, "KATIE, KATIE!" and nada. So, we walk on, and its cold in the dust now. I crouch down and touch it with my fingers. It's soft like quail pussy. Saltless and sanded down. We're drunk. We hear rabble. We yell out "CULLUM!?" And we yell it over and over and over again. And nada. We trudge in dirt red dust, sand mapped, nothing past fires and vans and dead dead death of the whole adventure. Death of the book death of the event. Nothing. "What are we doing man?" I ask. "I dunno," says Kial. We're glum. Gloomed out. Glib. And yeah. Well… what else… We walk. We walk. And we hear sounds near the canteen. That cowboy drink ticket and gamblers tuck-shop. We hear stuff going on. "Let's check it out," says Kial, and I damn sure agree. So, we do. He has no camera on him for once. I have a notebook. But man. I'm so sideways, I can't write my name. We walk up. Music blares. Bad music. Pop-Country. Deadly. Deadly Unna. We walk up and there's folks in cowboy hats and cowboy boots, men and women, all around and it's off and it's real and blaring and fucking hell. We step up the hill onto the concrete canteen. It's lit with white clinical lights, a horrorshow of free pouring boys and girls and men and women. An ocean again of plaid shirts and dusty jeans and a fishnet full of crawling cracking cowboy hat crustacean racing creeps. We look at the bar and all the rollers are up. There's no gap between the ticket spot and the drink purchase spot. It's all free range and there's bottles of Beam and Johnnie Red and two-liter cokes everywhere and of course the beloved putrid pipe-cleaning Bundy. So much Bundy. There're a couple of girls at the bar getting drinks, and the person pouring is the tall cowboy kid, Big Dick Energy. What is going on here? I look at Kial. "Drink?" "Yeah," and we both eye off the bottle of Beam on the counter so easily pinched… we could grab it and disappear into the night and nobody would be the wiser… Sit under the stars in the middle of the track and talk all night about unattainable dreams and what friendship really means. "Alright..." I lean into the bar, "Can I grab a Bundy and coke, mate?" "Yeah," says Big Dick Energy. He free-pours into a plastic cup and hands it to me. I sip it. He asks Kial what he wants. He says the same. And he gets it and we sip and then BDE takes an order from a girl behind us. That's it. It's free. It's an open bar... It's an OPEN bar. Jackpot. I guess we're hanging with the crew now, somehow... That was easy. This is something.

✱✱✱
The Rushes

Looking around with a plastic cup clutched in my hand I wonder what we're doing here. Drinking. Soaking whatever this is in. Is this a story? It is because I've decided that it is. I decided prior to Kial buying our Qantas tickets. I decided long ago, that whatever this was, was going to be a story. Kial and I stand around side by side. I start talking to a guy with a moustache who stands out amongst the yee-haw types. He's from Melbourne, travelling around and ended up here. That's fuckin weird. He's late twenties, wearing some kind of brown paisley pattern cardigan. He seems fine, bit weird, but whatever. And he says there's a lack of hot chicks here, but he's been on a tear throughout Australia, sleeping with a slew of women. I guess that's his schtick or whatever. Anther odd sort of short thin dude with a gaping grin enters our conversation, talks to us both but a little more at me. At me.

The brown cardigan wanders off. This dude I'm now speaking to has a Thirsty Camel cap on. Turns out he's a rep and gets sent out to events like this to sell booze and party with folks. Seems like some kind of life. Not a great one. How tiring, but he's all dumb smiles and he's short and looks up at me like a puppy dog and though he isn't threatening like I notice with most of the other burly big doggers now surrounding us here, who'd be all wearing MAGA hats if we were in the U.S, even so, he makes me squirm a bit. A young girl at the bar is drinking a vodka-soda and she's all dolled in a pink cowboy hat and rhinestone studded jeans and a light pink blouse. She's got pretty hefty tits on her but doesn't look all that mature. "This is crazy right?" she says to me. "Yeah, it's pretty wild. What are you doing here? You work here?" "Nah, my mum's here. Her friend organised it. So, I'm just with her and I'm having a few drinks haha! She doesn't mind, but doesn't want me to drink too much. But whatever! Haha!" "Yeah, right. Did you see the races?" "Yeah! So crazy! It's so much fun!" I get the distinct feeling she's not of age. Nah, fuck this. I dart around, fucking hell, I gotta leave this conversation. This is bait. I'm getting outta this one, "You have fun yeah," I say.

There's a group sitting on outdoor chairs in a semi-circle and a lot of fellas standing around them. The few women here seem to be sitting there. There's a couple of children running round too. Mostly there's carparks worth of huge boys standing around in cowdee hats and boots, swigging Bundy and eyeballing us. Nowhere seems all too inviting, but there's a dart board and the thing to do seems to partake in an activity to ease up tension. I recognise the camel racer girl we photographed before by the caravans. I mosey on over. She's darting with the creepy little Thirsty Camel rep. Kial sits on a steel rail that formed a queue to the canteen during the day. "You wanna play?" says Camel Breath rep with his camel breath. "Yeah, let's have a game. Kial? You and me vs them?" "Nah, I'll watch," He says. The camel racer and I talk about the obvious racing of the camels. She's always been into extreme sports but I'm not sure I'd call it one myself. She's had a load of injuries, broken legs, arms, ribs etc. from racing dirt bikes and whatever. I still dunno how she ended up racing camels and maybe neither does she. She's fine though. She seems a little on edge round here, but much friendlier than during the day. We shoot darts and I need more drinks and hit the bar again and again and again. Every time Kial and I look up from a conversation, there seems to be big drunken eyes tumbling over us like lint rollers, stickily picking up every hair and thread clinging to our clothes and bodies. I say 'hi' to a few folks sitting on plastic chairs. The response varies between acceptance and revolt. It's hard to know where the hell we stand here. There seems to be some great divergence between these people and us and them and each other. Like a thick rope across the dirt sand. We're loading up on drinks and there's a lot of wayward testosterone and conversation is off with everyone we chat with. But the free drinks are good, good enough to have us stay and see what happens, if anything happens. But it feels as though if something were to happen it wouldn't be good.

It doesn't take long to realise that all these big trucker-driving, cow-herding, gyrocopter flying type blokes are giving us head to toe hatred. Feels fucking weird. I'm in a trench coat, alright, I get it, but fucksake. We find ourselves talking to the rep again, is he following me around? There's this young fella in a cowboy hat who's talking to me and Kial and his colourful shirt is wide open. He asks us what we're doing here. We tell him that we dunno. "We're photographing the event for our own reasons really. I'm writing a piece on it." "Oh wow, that's cool." "You?" "I just come to events like this. Good to meet people and have a dance. Good music and that." "Yeah, right." This big burler behind him looks at Kial and grunts, "You right mate!?" Kial looks at him quizzically. He nods and lifts his drink. We keep talking to the young guy. Steering clear of the heifers. We shuffle around trying to find somewhere to stand. Near the dartboard a beef-faced guy stares at me then, "What are you?" I look at him. "Urgh, I'm a writer mate." He scoffs and chuckles into his pork-loin faced friend's ear. The place is a butchery. Fucking prick. I head to the bar. I'm fucking wasted now. This drinking has been going all day, all last few days. Morning till night. And within the last hour it's scaled up relentlessly with free pouring undiluted bourbon and Bundy and shit beer brewed in the Queen's land. With BDE slinging drinks and drinking himself he feels like some sort of safe-zone with his wide brimmed cowdee hat under sharp lighting. The bar is always a safe-zone. He seems to understand the situation. More than we do anyway. It's clear he's a kid but for whatever reason nobody seems to mess with him. He's young, but he's got some sort of golden child thing about him. If it was America he'd be the star quarter back and the prom king sort of thing. We lean in and chat. We talk a little about whatever and I see that Brown Cardigan fella chatting to the young girl. He won't leave her alone. I bet she's underage and I bet he doesn't care. BDE catches me looking. "She pretty hot huh? Be careful. She's 14 and her mums just there." He points to a sinewy woman with sunken cheeks sitting on a plastic chair by a pram, her head is on loose, neck like rubber. Shaking off some feeling like the smell of sour milk. "Yeah, no shit. 14 though? God. Could have gotten into trouble for a minute." He nods. "You boys want some Ritalin? Kial and I look at each other. "Ah, yeah. Sure." "Alright." He bends down behind the bar. I turn to Kial, "Perfect." "Yeah, what are the chances?" "This is good at least. Everything else happening feels a bit fucked." "Yeah I know. It's like everyone here wants us dead." "And that girl, man. She was coming right at me. I didn't know what to make of that. You think that dude knows she's 14 and he just doesn't care or what?" "I dunno. Bit of a creep." "Yeah man." BDE gives us a pill each. "Just one?" "Yeah, one's fine man. Thanks heaps. How'd you get em?" "I get them prescribed, I have ADHD, so they help. I was fucking crazy before these. Like, fucking crazy mate." "Yeah, sweet. Thanks." Kial and I tap our pills together and down em with fresh pool cleaner. We meander further into the swamp of people getting dirt-eyed at every moment. These bastards. They're all bastards. Amongst the sneers and cachinnation, one big mate shouts, "Let's have a Goanna Pull!? Eh? You heard of one of those, mate?!" bursts a bloated and upside-down crocodile carcass of a bastard. Right in my face. He snarls. He smirks. He looks around at all the other sausage faced and gristle eyed freaks and they laugh and cheer. They raise their cups and shout and holler dumb fucking noises that reverberate in the shed and canteen and brim to the track and shake the ground. What on earth is happening... "Nah, I haven't. What is it?" We tie a belt round ya neck and another blokes neck and you get on all fours and you pull. The winner is the one that pulls the other one over the line." I look at him. "Pfft. Whatever man," I say. He's surely just made this thing up. Fuck this guy. "You and yer mate do it!" Says fellow fat-rancher. I look up and around.

"You and him! You and him!" another points. "Ah, right. Nah man, haha. I reckon you do it and I'll have a think about it." I say slowly backing away towards the bar. I laugh it off. Shrug it off. These guys are just playing a game with out-of-towners. Someone else chimes in slurring through a XXXX tin, "Yeah! You and ya girl-mate do it! Haha!" Someone nudges Kial, "Go on do it." "Nope, fuck that. You fucking do it." Kial says. "He won't fuckin do it! Hahaha!" The hordes of heaving ham laugh belly beer laughs. You can hear the froth sloshing in their guts when their cracked lips open. I catch the look of an ogre of a man in black who's been sitting by the woman that all the other plastic chairs seem to encircle like an outback concrete-canteen throne. He's not laughing and he's not smiling. All the smaller men seem to be weaving in and out of the big hefty guy's legs or they've scampered to the toilets or they're hiding under chairs. Everything seems hazy and drunk and I'm losing touch. The woman on the concrete-canteen throne wears a big weather worn Akubra that tilts over her face. Since glancing that way, the big fella in black has felt like a stockade between her and her female friend, the mother of the young girl. The ogre in black with a punisher T-shirt is a wall between the Empress and the salivating bull inseminating beef boned battering rams that stomp and cackle about like bulls in a pen. Shoulder to shoulder. Deep laughter coming from all around and colliding to form a deeper quakier sound. The ogre raises his fat paw. "Alright, Alright I'll do it!" The little camel breather leers at me from under the wing of a botched hippo, "It happens everywhere. It's a tradition. You really haven't heard of it before?" He squeals. Fucking freak. "Nah, I haven't. Sounds fucking weird, man." "It's not, haha. It's not." The Ogre has dusty blonde receding hair and a shit sandy stubble smirk. I move towards the bar, to BDE. "Man, this seems fucking weird." "Yeah? You haven't seen or heard of it before?" He smiles. "Mate, it's tradition. Don't listen to those guys. We all do it." He seems earnest. What the fuck? "Yeah, right." I say. "You should give it a go. Specially if you haven't done it. It's a bit of fun. Just watch." He points. Another big boy in a brown t-shirt with cow udder guts puts his hand up. "I'll take ya on!" Everyone claps their callous mitts. The few women here in the cold country air are laughing. The blokes are laughing. BDE leaps over the bar. "Alright. Alright! I got the belt fellas!" He announces as he whips his leather belt off from around his waist. He ties it into a loop and holds it up like a championship. "You know the rules! Here's the line!" He points the toe of his cowboy boot along a crease in the concrete. "First one pulled over this line loses! We got any bets?!!" Everyone laughs. The Ogre and the big bloated boar get on their hands and knees. I look at Kial. He's sipping his drink with his aviators on perched on another railing, out of the action but taking every little drop of oddity in. BDE in his striped blue shirt, bung eyed on country pharma in his cowdee hat places the belt round the thick bullish necks of these two fat men on their hands and knees. They yank back at each other to make sure it's in place. "Alright! Alright! Wait for the count! Wait for the count!" All pressure of the belt at the back of their necks. They're facing each other, strangely intimate and vulnerable but still loaded with wrangler aggression, testosterone, ferocity, XXXX and Bundy. "3, 2, 1, GO!" BDE shouts and swings off his hat. The big boys start grunting. Their faces go boiled yabby red. Pulling their greasy-bottomed-Maccas-bag-bodies away from each other. The belt wriggles around their flabby necks. Their teeth bared. Grunt. Grunt. Grunt. The drunk hoard cheers and claps. Their hands and knuckles whiten on the cold concrete floor taking the pressure of their beached fish bodies. Heave. Heave. Heave. The big security looking motherfucker, the ogre, blue eyed and somewhat sympatico in comparison to these steak grilling gorillas, gives a huge backed-up mighty yank and his opponent buckles at the elbows and falls across the line. He raises his hands in the air, on his knees, and roars! "Yeeahh!!" The loser, shaking his head, gets to one knee, and some other fatty helps him up. The winning oafy ogre stands up and takes the belt off from around his neck. Everyone shouts and cheers. BDE turns to me. "You wanna go mate? C'mon." But he didn't care either way. He wasn't applying pressure like the ominous crowd had. Another bloke points at Kial, "You two do it!" The guys laugh again. "Hey! Settle will ya!" says BDE. "Don't worry bout these blokes!" Then he turns to us, "Don't take it personally." "Yeah, fuck it. I'll do it," I say. Some crap filled motherfucker in a red T says, "I'll take him!" and he literally rubs his hands together. "Fuck off mate! You'll fucking kill me!" I shout. The blokes laugh, and he stares at me like I'm a stick of jerky stuck in his teeth. The Brown Cardigan raises his hand and gives a look to the 14 year old ranch girl standing to the side of him. "I'll do it!" He claps his hands to get amped up. This is fairer. We're about the same height and there's not a drip of outback in either of us. "Alright, you and me," I say. The farting crowd cheer and fuckin fart and swamp themselves in a revolting air of riff raff and hollerings. "Alright, you fellas ready?" BDE asks quietly. "Yeah." "Yeah." BDE waves the belt in the air. "Alright, alright ladies and gentlemen! We have another Goanna Pull!" he leans to me, "Sloan, yeah?" He asks the other guy who looks uncomfortably similar to me now that I'm face to face with him, and he says whatever his pedo-ey name is. "We have Sloan VS (Brown Cardigan?)" The crowd roar and holla like Midwestern fratboys in a strip club. "Down on your hands and knees fellas," he says. I take off my coat and hand it to Kial. Kial shakes his head. I get down on my hands and knees. The concrete is cold. I can smell the dust and the grass just over the edge of the canteen. I can smell leather boots and beer. I look back to Kial and take a deep perplexed breath of the strange fresh air and the filth crude of cowboy bastards. Kial shakes his head again. I shake mine. I look at my opponent, he's shaking his head too. What the fuck is going on? BDE places the belt round our necks. "Are you ready!" Fuck, this is pretty gay. The crowd yee-haws and farts and burps and all that fucking shit. "3, 2, 1, PULL!" I go in hard, fast and pull at him, he is biting his lip and reddening. He's twisting his neck around. I feel the belt on the back of mine and the hard floor on my knee caps. Fuck this. I heave. He heaves back. Eye contact in this situation is gross. I can't deal with it. I have to end it. End this sleezebags bravado. But in what a way. I pull back hard on the secretive pedo and his hand slips over the line. "WE HAVE A WINNER LADIES AND GENTLEMEN!!" BDE waves his cowboy hat in the air. Thank fuck. Amongst the roar, I get to my feet quickly, and check the back of me, I take the belt off. I remember Katie asking me if I'd seen a Goanna Pull yet just that day come to think of it. Fucking hell. At least I won. I shake hands and pat Brown Cardigan on the back. He isn't all that bad apart from his morals. BDE announces another one and asks for participants. Camel Breath raises his hand with a bubbly little piss drinking grin and Brown Cardigan goes in for round two to impress his child bride no doubt. Me and Kial go pour ourselves drinks form the bar as the crowd surround the next Goanna Pull. "How was that?" "Fuck, man. I dunno. Pretty fucked up. I just felt like I had to win you know? This is all too weird. I dunno why I did that. Ease the tension? It was pretty gay dude." "Yeah, I know. Whatever that was, that was one of the most insane things I've ever seen." "Yeah, right?" I need a drink bad. "What the fuck man," I say again. We drink our shoe polish water back quickly. Then pour ourselves more. And there's more Goanna Pulls with the open shirt kid and some other guys. And one dude with a blonde mullet and glasses who looks like he's going to a dress up party and the theme is molestation. He's one of the slimiest creepiest fucking things I've seen.

Eventually, the crowd dispels clapping and the drunk beasts take their plastic seats again and BDE leaps back over the bar to drink and pour more for others now thirstier than before. We ask him for another two Ritalin and snack em back. He's glad to hand them out to us, but I don't see him telling anyone else. The energy around us in this concrete shed canteen is amped up. Goanna Pulls get the crowd going I guess. And the eyes on us are a little seedier, like they're all in on a joke or something. The tension certainly did not ease. All these men. All these men are somehow threatened by us. What are we doing to them. We're under their alligator skin. I lean to Kial, "Man, should I say something about that Brown Cardigan guy? He's trying to pick up that 14-year-old so blatantly. I feel fucking torn here. Her mum's here. But, what do we do?" "I dunno. I mean, her mum's here, right? I know what you mean, but he hasn't done anything has he?" "Nah, but like… I dunno. This is all fucking weird. He seemed relatively normal at first." "Nah, he's fucked. They're all insane."

I get another drink and walking away from the bar a 6"4 semi-trailer bastard spits, "HEY!" "Yeah mate?" I say. "You fags or what?" "What?" "Hey, hey, hey. Its' just a fucking question. Are you a faggot? Do ya like boyyyys?" giggles the fat snarling fuck. His lips quiver with confrontational ecstasy. "Maybe I am? Maybe I'm not? How's that make you feel?" "Woah, woah. So, you are a faggot are ya?" Getting angry, I spit back, "Mate, I might just be a fucking faggot! You like that?" He lunges at me quick for a god damn walking chicken kiev, full of melted dairy and crumbed round the edges by his own ideals, spilling his drink a bit, his face has curled up, tiny sunburnt lips, face like a pink pig's butthole. His step toward me is halted by another big boy behind him. "HEY, HEY! Fucking stop it mate! Let em be! They aren't hurting anyone!" I stare at the big boy. I fucking stare right at him. And he stares back. I don't feel 4"5 anymore. I feel like I could smack the gristle outta his mouth. He gives me a prison shower smirk. "Fucking leave him mate!" His friend shouts, and a few other cowboys stand up, stopping the escalation. What on earth is this fucking bullshit. I look around again but with some clarity from the Ritalin. I walk back over to the table where Kial had been chatting with Camel Breath and the boy with the open shirt. I could hear the plastic chair Empress freaking out about the kid with his shirt open. "You right?" asks the kid. "Yeah man, fucking hell. What was that about?" "Yeah, I dunno. These events can be strange." I sip my drink and shake it off. He continues, "So, are you gay?" I roll my eyes. "Why?" "I don't know." He says. "Look, it doesn't matter. Whatever is whatever. Why does everybody need to know? Sexuality is a spectrum man, I like whoever I like." "Yeah, yeah. Look, it's a nice night, you want to take a walk for a bit, check out the tracks?" he asks softly. What is happening here? I ask myself again and again. He's looking into my eyes. His shirt is undone. His chest is bare and white. "Umm... maybe later…" "Ok, we can just take a little walk?" says the cowboy kid. "Ok, well, yeah I'll let you know," I say. If I walk out along the track with him it could be a trick. I could get jumped and beat. Or maybe fucked by him and a bunch of other dudes hanging out for it here. "Just a walk," he smiles and goes on, "We can just go round there?" I could just get my dick sucked. That'd be something and it'd be a 'fuck you' to the fatty deposit cattlemen. I look at his cowboy hat. Wait but would it? In the dark I wouldn't have to look at the kid. Or maybe I would? Katie didn't work out. This kids 18. He's 18? How badly do I want a blowjob? Oh man, pretty bad I guess. "Ok, ok. Let's take a walk. I just gotta take a piss. I'll be back." Jesus fuck. Would I fuck his ass? Would he fuck my ass? Nah, nah. Would I touch his cock? He had no stubble. How would he suck me off? I imagine his fleshy pink asshole and his stiff young cattle rearing cock, bent up and pink, tipple of semen at the eye like a ready and weighty udder. The weight and throb of it in my hand and his course palm around mine. This is all a lot right now. I'd be putting my money where my mouth is. Well not just my money. I walk around the corner and take a piss and breathe frosty outback air waiting for a clear and concise thought. I don't fucking want that kid to suck me off. Nah. Nope. I come back to the shed and he's chatting to someone else and I slip right by him. I don't want his lips round my dick with his open shirt and his cowboy hat bobbing up and down on my pole. I don't want that boy sucking on my dick. No, nope. No thanks. I struggle to say no to a lot of things. Even now, I'm not saying no. I turn around. I look at Kial who's deeper amongst the folks than me, still sitting on a rail sipping his drink in a plastic cup, taking the mayhem in through his aviators. Suddenly the mullet molester whips Kial's sunglasses off him and giggles. Mullet molester starts quivering with macabre glee, hucking through his buck teeth, fogging up his thick square prescription glasses, and Kial's staring this horror movie uncle down the barrel. I expect the pedo to start doing a jig. Kial gets down off the rail and snatches his sunglasses back, saying something to the effect of, "Don't fucking do that again," and the molester laughs it off, giggles even, like it's a schoolyard game. He's testing who takes bottom and who takes top. These dirty big cowboy blokes are testing us. The night feels darker than it did before. The betting, the racing, the highs are still being chased. Everyone is a rabid thing from somewhere across this desert. I feel like Querelle, but I'm not rolling dice. And the Empress bitch? Who is she in all of this? Everything else is clear as day now in pitch black nowhere. Cowboy heels click and scrape on the floor of a concrete shed, chortling echoes and guttural groans rumble round the corrugated tin roof spat out into the deep starry abyss of indifferent Channel Country like semen in the Milky Way. And the shit country music plays on and on.

****
Plastic Chair Republic

Kial tells me about the hick freak that grabbed his glasses. "Yeah I saw him. Jeeze, man. I'll get us some more drinks." The energy seems to have shifted over to a different corner of the canteen. Kial and I are out of the way now. If we stand around the bar, for the most part, we are out of the firing line. Amongst all the discomfort and it still feels good to hop the bar and pour our own. All the beers in the fridge are middies, so there's no drinking them really, there's no point. I make two strong mop bucket waters and feel the sugar coating my teeth and tongue like clag. I come back to Kial who's leaning against the shed wall. "Did you see that shit?" "Nah, what?" "You know how that boss lady sitting on the plastic chairs was carrying on about that kid she didn't like?" "Yeah, something to do with his open shirt or something?" "Yeah, she kept saying, 'I don't want him here! I don't want him here!' hysterical and dramatic. Then that big Goanna Pull guy, who looks like her personal security or something went up to him and I thought he was gonna pick him up and strangle him. He took him outside and I thought he was gonna kick the shit out of him, bash him or something. I didn't know what I could do, he's huge and there's so many people here and that guy was just a kid with an open shirt."

"Yeah, shit. What happened?" "He just took him away, got up real close to him and had a stern chat. I think he told him to button up his shirt or something and fuck off outta here, but he just talked to him and walked away. He went from looking like he was about to beat this kid to death to being a sort of sweetheart to him." "What the fuck? That's weird." "Yeah, fucking strange." "Well, that kid was just asking me to take a walk with him before." "What? The kid with the open shirt?" "Yeah, man. You should have seen his eyes. The gall too. What is going on man? I'm being called a faggot and then this kid asks me to go off in the darkness with him. I almost did just to see what would happen. But it was pretty obvious what was gonna happen." "Damn. This whole thing is making me feel so uncomfortable." "Yeah, fucking hell. I mean, I wanna hang around and see it out though. There's unlimited alcohol." "No, definitely. Me too." I decided to piss in the toilets. I walked in and heard grunting coming from a cubicle as I shipped my junk out and aimed it at the piss tray. Oh, fuck this. I went to the other cubicle and tried to lock the door. It wouldn't lock. I pulled myself out again and looked at the toilet roll dispenser. There was an open and empty baggy there. Pills or MD for sure. How many of these dudes are just gacked or methed or something? Everyone looked fried in some way, from trauma, repressed sexuality, an abundance of testosterone, pedophilic urges. Whatever it was it wasn't drug fueled, just maybe, here and there drug accompanied. And usually when drugs are around, they find their way to me – hence the Ritalin. They seek me out like buzzing little bees to pollen. Drugs know I'm the prettiest flower in the garden. But instead of drugs, it was bulldozer outback jacks. The I'm not gay but you's a faggot sorta things. There was a strong sense of rape coming off the meat-tray fellas too. Like, call you a faggot and fuck you up the ass sort of rape. And that mum of the young girl with the rubber neck and eyes rolling back in paralyzing ecstasy. It makes more sense now and all we've had is Ritalin. I leave pretty quick with all my bits tucked away and go back to Kial who just turned to me from talking to a girl and a guy who weren't quite as shitfaced as the rest were getting. "Just saw a baggy in the toilets and heard grunting," I say. "Fuck! I just shook hands with those two and they said, 'you've got a cold hand' in a really confrontational way like they were implying something." "Fucking hell. You wanna sit down?" "Yeah, you sit, I'll grab another drink. I'll hop the bar again." Returning, "Yeah, I know. Fucking mental." And I give Kial a drink. I should speak to this Empress woman. I wanna sit down and all the seats are around her. There seems to be a small amount of intoxicated peace in her presence despite her shouting and screaming about that kid. But who knows what he did. "Kial, I'm gonna go sit over there. Looks like everyone thinks she's important for some reason. Wanna join?" "Nah, I'm fine here. Maybe later." I enter the plastic chair semi-circle, the republic of Camel County. "Can I sit here?" I ask the Empress. She eyes me up and down. Her Akubra still pulled down mighty. "Yeah." She says. "How ya doing?" I ask. "What are you doing here?" she spurs. "Errr... yeah. I'm writing a piece on the event and my mate's been photographing it." "You work for someone? I didn't hire you, did I?" "No, it's our own project. We sort of cover subcultural events, but approach it differently, aesthetically rather than journalistically, you know?" "Right. What do you mean?" "Umm... I guess. The journalism stuff doesn't really motivate us. Anyone can say this and that happened and give a clean-cut redelivery of events. But, this is through our own lens. The racing takes a back seat to the experience of being here and witnessing it." "Why would you do that? What's fucking here?" "I mean, this... this is pretty fucking weird for us." The huge ogre now leans over. He's sitting opposite me, I see his big meat feet pressing into his dusty sandals. "That's enough, yeah. Leave her alone" "What?" I say. "Nah, he's alright. Leave him," she tells the oaf. I'm pretty fucking perplexed again. Kial returns to his spot on the rail uncertain about joining the social confusion down here. "That's what you two are doing here? Writing a story?" she asks. "Yeah, well. I'm writing it. He's photographing." Some guy near us on one of the chairs says, "Any money you's make, make sure you remember us ey?" "Yeah, sure." I tell him sarcastically. The Empress waves her hand dismissively. She's wearing a long dark duster. The gacked mum is sitting next to her. She suddenly pipes up out of her MD brain fizzle and says, "You should write a story about this one's life. It's fuckingggg crazy. Best seller there." "Oh really?" I say with forced fucking sincerity. Never ever tell a writer that they should write a bio on your fucking friend. I mean, c'mon. The Empress sparks a Winfield blue and a blob of a bloke near me asks her if he can have one, "No, fuckin get your own you scab" she spits. Her friend continues, "She's been through some shit, me and her," she drools and slops over, rocking the pram next to her. "What's in there?" I ask. "My kid, the fuck you reckon?" and she opens it up and looks in. There's a baby in there alright wrapped up tight in a blanket. "Ah right." "Can't leave her in the tent and the fucking dad dun do shit so, what am I gonna do?" she reasons. "Right." "You got kids?" She asks with disdain. An embittered seething ghost crawls out of her twisted mouth. "No, no rush." "Yeah, I fucking bet ey!" she laughs to herself with a lolling tongue. The whites of her bloodshot eyes seem to buzz with static and one eye bobs around in her socket like loose change, the gacked cunt. "So, what? You just write stories and go around the outback?" asks the Empress and Gackle's head starts rolling round on that rubber neck again. "Nah, I study. We just do this sort of thing when we can." "Oh yeah, an intellectual are ya? What are you studying? At Uni?" "Not an intellectual, no. But, yeah, I'm at Uni. I'm doing a masters in philosophy." I realise everyone else on the chairs has been listening to us speak when gasps escape from numerous directions. The oafy ogre leans forward on his chair and his eyebrows furrow with deep and difficult contemplation. "PHILOSOPHY! Why you doin that?!" he thunders. "Urgh, well, I mean, I want to understand my existence as best I can. On a human level. My focus is on existentialism and aesthetics. Like, through aesthetics I think there's some clue to understanding human connection and meaning. I think without art and creativity we can never really understand each other. We keep trying to assert opinions as truth on each other. And you can never know what anyone else is thinking, you can never really trust anyone because they're caught up in trying to protect themselves all the time. People don't mean to be dishonest, but if you're lying to yourself, you lie to everyone around you. The only way any truth gets through is when you can openly express it through an artform or through aesthetics…" Everyone is quiet, I don't know why I'm talking, but I continue, "Because in art, you get the opportunity to be honest with yourself, and people fuck that up too, don't get me wrong. But it's the only situation where that honesty is available. I mean… I think so. That's what my thesis is on. Nothing is guaranteed to mean anything. It's what you make of it." The silence is chilling amongst the plastic chair republic. "What the fuck did you just even say?" says the rubberneck, her head now totally unattached from her spine. "Yeah, I dunno. Nevermind." I shake my head. I went too far. "So, you're a deep guy? You're a thinker?" says the oaf, and he smiles at me and his blue eyes light up. He continues, "I like you. You're alright. So, you're saying life has no meaning?" he slurs, heavy, heavy with his breath. "I mean, you create your own meaning. There's no great plan to fall back on. It's on you to create purpose." "So, life's shit?" the Empress asks. "No, no, it's the opposite. It is what it is right? We're here. What are we gonna do about it? We can be pretty certain we are all in this together, right?" Silence. Then she says, "Hmmm… I like you. You've got a good head on ya. My life's shit you know. I organised all of this! I run all of this. I put all the money in. I made all this happen. I have thousands of cattle. This bar behind me is all on me, cause I don't give a fuck. I want everyone to enjoy themselves. I don't have a husband anymore cause he's a cunt and when he left I became more successful without him. But none of it's worth anything. It's worth nothing to me." "Yeah, right." I say, and add, "That's it. There is no meaning in that stuff. You're following on from what's expected of you and you're obviously doing a damn good job of it, but what do you want? What is real purpose to you?" Another silence. "Fuck," says the oaf nodding. And the other big boys round me squirm in their plastic chairs. "Fuck this. What's the point of that!?" one mutters. "That's it, man. I don't fucking know." Boss Bitch nods in reflection. The gacked bitch seems to be sobering and she's staring at me weighing me up and Oafy has a huge smile cracking across his dumb gentle face. The other blokes shift in their seats and get up, one says something about me being full of shit and they disperse to the bar. "You want a cigarette?" asks the Empress. "Yeah, thanks, I've got one rollie left and I've been saving it." "Anytime you want a smoke, just ask," she says. "You know, I could tell you were intelligent. You can tell by someone's face," says Oafy. "Your nose and eyes. I mean I wouldn't be wearing what you are here. But I could tell you were a thinker." "Thanks." I shrug uncomfortably. "What do you think of me?" he asks. I'm taken back. "Like, what you reckon?" he persists. "Um… What do you mean?" "You're smart. Tell me what you see!" "Urgh, ok. Well, you obviously seem pretty fucking intimidating initially. Like, you're a big scary fucking dude. But sitting here and looking into your eyes. They're gentle. You're actually full of kindness. I can see that. You're soft, obviously mean when you need to be.

But not as mean as you make out right?" He looks at me like a bear with a thorn in his paw. "Yeah, you're right you know." "Yeah, he's a just a big softy," says the Empress. "You seem like you've known each other a long time or something?" I say to them. "Nah, it's strange, we just met the other day and I told him to come work for me here. He's kind of my personal security. He does what I say." "Right. Weird." "Me and her just clicked. Got along well right away." Oafy says, and I see Gackles jiggle her cup, calling for her daughter to come over and fill-er-up. The girl comes over all busty Peggie-Sue, "You been drinking too much?" asks mum. "No, just a few." "You sure? Don't get drunk now, yeah?" "I know, I know." "Get mum another vodka lemonade wouldja?" "Alright." She smiles and wobbles her plump 14-year-old ass over to the bar where Brown Cardigan is still clinging. "You seeing that guy chatting to her all night?" I say to Gackles. "Yeah, yeah I know. But, fuckin, she's gotta learn somehow. I got knocked up young. I didn't learn. She's gotta know, right?" "What do you mean?" "Boys, ya dickhead! Men. She's gonna learn one way or another, and I'd rather be around than her off somewhere else with em." I nod and give a sort of meh reaction to her response. From that point she starts opening up to me more and is getting a little charmed by me for some reason. The MD or whatever is wearing off and she's a touch coherent. I find myself wondering, would I? Nah, she's fucked, wrinkled. There's literally a baby in the pram beside her. The Empress? Hmmm, now maybe. She isn't much to look at. But nothing here is. But why anyone? Why am I thinking like this? Would I? Yeah, I would. Would I try for it though? No, no I wouldn't. Am I absorbing the purpose of this midnight canteen soirée? And we talk more. And Boss Bitch and her friend and I and Oafy are getting on fine and they're alright actually. Some guys send some more bullshit words my way, and the Empress Boss Bitch straight up tells them to shut the fuck up and fuck off. What the obsession with me is, is still confusing. I narrow it down to my soft features and my trench coat. And probably my stubbornness to refuse any answers regarding my sexuality. These are big men. These are tractor sized men. She doesn't give a fuck. Whatever this hell hole is, she's King Bitch here. And I'm on her right-hand side, and I'm the only one she's giving cigarettes out to. "Kial, Kial!" I call him over. "Hey, how's it goin?" he asks with a hand in his pocket and his sunnies still on. "You're the photographer?" says King Bitch. "Yeah, I guess you could say that." Everyone shakes hands with him and Gackles bats her thin cigarette singed eyelashes at him. We're now all in the plastic chair circle, the plastic chair republic, with King Bitch at the throne. Oafy on the left. Me on her right. Her best friend and the baby on an angle on her right too and

Kial on my right, one spot down from Oafy on the opposite side. Around us men bump and slap each other, some wrestle on the wet grassy hill down from us, there's spitting and sculling of drinks and yelling and BDE comes over every now and then and asks us how we are and we talk and he goes back to the bar again to do whatever ADHD shit he was doing before. Are we still in the *Rushes*? Where's the anti/sublimated faggotism? Where're the threats? Where are the boys on walks? Are they walking or in the cubicle? Have they sorted out tops and bottoms and the rest are just fooling about? "If you get any shit from anyone here. Look at me. If anyone gives you any problems. You tell me, ok?" says Oafy to the both of us with grave sincerity. "Thanks mate." "No, thank you. I've never met guys like you two. You understand me." "Well, thanks." And King Boss Bitch says, "Yeah, I've never met anyone like you, you know. I can talk to you." And I turn toward her and we get talking more, one on one and her friend gets up and needs to stretch or some shit. King Bitch is telling me all her woes, her life story, from this to that, to husbands and kids and money and the outback and the country and her sadness. All her infinite sadness. And I'm telling her she's Ok. And that she's a good person and shit like that and through this talk she takes a break to piss and she pisses with her friend in the toilets and Oafy leans into me on his plastic chair again and he says,

"Stop that. I'm telling you. You need to stop that now!" His sudden change of demeanor is a little concerning but I also know he thinks I've seen into his soul now. He respects me, despite being half his height and probably a quarter his weight. "What?" "You're trying too hard. You're scaring her off. Stop it." I laugh and say, "I'm not trying anything. I'm just talking." He shakes his head. He gives me a scorn, almost a growl, like a fucking dog, a desert-bleached Rottweiler, maybe more like a pissed-on hog. "I'm not trying shit," I say. And he shakes his head like he knows better or something. Kial's sitting in the plastic republic very confused. The tension between Oafy and I quells as King Bitch comes back and takes her seat next to me. She smiles with reservation. She doesn't want to like me but she's probably fucking gacked. Maybe they went off to take more MD. How's the baby? God damn. A song comes on that's different to the Ute fuckery hick shit we've been listening to all night, and I start asking "Who has the phone?" and it looks like it's BDE. Oafy suddenly gets up and starts dancing like a walrus. The big ol boy is blissing out. He's wiggling his chonky ass around and I'm laughing and Kial's laughing and all the rest of the animals in this shed are laughing and some start dancing too. Kial says to me, "You see that chick with the moon boot before? She was a camel rider but fucked her leg. Hilarious, she was the best-looking girl here, easily, and had a moonboot on! Haha!" I laugh with him. "I don't think I saw her." "Ah, ha, I gave her my cowboy hat. I just plonked it on her head and we talked and now she's gone. I don't think I'm getting that hat back." And we laugh some more and we sip our urinal wash and we feel pretty fucking weird but pretty fucking drunk and very fucking intrigued by the whole thing that has and is unfolding. It must be damn late now. When does the sun come up? Whatever. I get that weird throb in my nervous system. Picture the red wires that fill your skin, no veins, just the electricity. All of that in me is now alight. I am brimming. Booze gets you to a certain point. If you drink enough and you don't puke and you don't pass out, you get a lightning bolt all the way through you. And that's when shit gets scary. That's when you can do anything. There's still a bar of drinks, free drinks, plenty, plenty free drinks. After convincing BDE to chuck on the Rolling Stones I see people going cross eyed and tight lipped with genuine confusion. Everyone's bored, including the plastic chair republic. The only person here that even recognises them is sweetheart Oafy. None of these bastards know where country comes from. They don't understand the link with the blues. They don't get nothing that isn't American Midwest top ten trash. I thought the Stones'd be middle ground. Wrong. Nobody knows shit about shit. I try a few more suggestions to meet them farther down the middle like Johnny Cash and Townes Van Zandt, but nothing is gluing, they want that pick-up truck Jack Daniels tribute stuff -

> Songs about birthing cows and
> square dancing with a toad
> On a Friday night
> Sipping warm Coors light
> Beneath the pale moon
> Sah bright
> Sah bright
> Gassin' down the drive in a chevvy
> Pa beatin' Ma on the levee
> Car go vroom
> Revy, revy

Idiots.

King Bitch is now looking sloppy. Gackles droopy. Oafy is a little unstable and there's a few others around still but I dunno who they are. Why am I alive? Ritalin. Thank you, King Bitch for accepting me into the plastic chair republic. I otherwise woulda been swallowed up in the canteen-*Rushes*. Taken for a walk or Goanna Pulled into a beefcakes asshole. Now there's vague drunk faces floating in country twang around me, receding midnight and dissipating testosterone. Thank fuck. Kial and I feel more at ease, and we've completely forgotten that the only thing holding us together is the Ritalin BDE gave us hours ago. Gackles is rocking her pram and now really enjoying Kial's blondie androgynous company. It's pretty clear she's hitting on him and I don't know what to make of that and King Bitch is really trying to get deep into me, conversationally. She's saying things like, "You're the only person for years that has understood me," and "I've never met anyone like you." She asks again, leaning in and down with her Akubra, "So, wait… what are you doing here again? I don't understand. Why?" "That's what I'm trying to find out. I'm just writing through it. It seemed like a wild and strange event. And it is. I have to live what I write. That's the sort of writer I am if I am one at all." "So, confusing," she says floating away into reflection. She gives me another cigarette and I thank her. I light hers, then mine and Oafy gives me a mean look. Stupid bigfoot, give it a break. Me and Kial turn to each other and the others start talking with each other. "She hitting on you?" I ask. "Yeah, I think that's what's happening." "It's getting light. What should we do?" "I dunno. I'm getting over this." "Yeah, me too." Then King Bitch announces quite matter of fact, "Alright, we're going for a cruise into town. Who wants to come?" Kial and I look at each other. Fuck. "Yeah, let's go, fuck it. This is probably the worst decision we could make. Everyone is totally fried. "Who's driving?" I ask. "I'll drive," says King Bitch. Fucking hell. "Yeah alright." Everyone stands up from the plastic half circle republic. And everyone else has gone home. The rushes are over? Only the inner sanctum is left and barely standing at that. Little wobbly. Pram and all. Oafy is shaking his head. He's got a sour look on his sunburnt face. "You don't wanna go with them," he rumbles. "Why? Yeah, nah we'll go. Fuck it." He shakes his heavy ogre head. "Ok." The republic start heading out to the gate, stumbling in their boot cut rhinestone studded jeans. "Let's get another drink quick." I say to Kial. "Yep." "I'll wait for you boys," says Oafy, who has now shifted his security role to us. "Cheers man." Kial and I jump the bar and pour some drinks for each other. Filled cups, we waltz out the canteen and down the bank. BDE hangs back to close it all up. The group left with a bottle of Jim Beam when they all shuffled off. We shoulda thought of that. Having just rushed a drink I felt a little woozy. "Can't believe they're going for a drive. Fuck, what's in town anyway at this time? What are they doing?" I say to Kial. "Yeah, fuck. We could die. This could be it." Says Kial, and continues, "I wouldn't even care. Seems right." "Yeah, I guess so. I mean. We die, we die. What a way to go. Trying to make something for ourselves, avoiding some rape and dying in a car accident in Boulia town." "Head on collision with a semi-trailer with a car full of drunk old women." "Yeah, seems fine." We walk up to Oafy, "So, where are they?" I ask. "Oh, they went down there." "Ok. So, what are they doing?" "Going for a drive," he says. "Yeah. But where are we meeting them?" "They're going for a drive," he repeats. Me and Kial walk on beside him. It's not quite light yet. Its looming, but the darkness is very much all around. "Where are they?" I ask again, I turn around, doing a 360 and I'm pretty mentally messed, that Ritalin is slipping off. "Hey, hey, it's alright. Calm down. They're fine. Just slow down," Oafy says to us. Kial and I look at each other. Oafy's shoulders lift up, palms open to the moon. He offers us only a perplexed shrug. "Yeah, but we'll miss them?" I say. "Would they have gone down there?" Kial points. "Hey, hey! Look, let's just sit down and have a cigarette. We won't catch up to them now." says Oaf. "What?" "We've missed them, don't you realise. And we won't catch up. Just let it go Sloan. You've been trying to control things all night. Asking so many questions. Your mind races too much. You need to learn to stop thinking so much. And just cool down." "I don't think too much. What are you talking about?" "See, you just asked another question. You're stuck in your head." "That doesn't make sense. I'm thinking just as much as you are only about different things." "See what I mean," he says with drunk consideration. "Ok, so we've lost them?" "They've gone. Don't you understand? They've left without you." "Ok, ok. Whatever." I light my last cigarette. Kial is looking around. The sun is barely making any effort to morning this red shit part of the planet. We get outside the gates and Oafy stops and puts his hand on my chest so I'd stop too. "That's my truck there." He whispers, "Now… I have a bed in there. I can sleep one of you's, but not both. So, if you like, one of you can stay, but the other will have to go. You can figure it out between you." I look at his fucking fat dusty Sasquatchean feet. Then I look at him in his soft-hearted submissive face, once again. "Huh?" I say. "I only have room for one. I can fit one of you's, but the other will have to go." I look at Kial. Kial looks at me. I look at Oafy's putrid fucking sapphire eyeballs. You cunt. You fucking cunt. "Nah, nah. We have a tent. We're fine." "Well, I can fit one of you's with me and the other can go to the tent." "Nah, we're staying together." "I can fit one." "Nah, we'll just go to our tent together. It's a good tent. We're fine. Don't worry." "Ok. Well?" he drops. "Yeah, look. We are fine Ok." "But, you guys…" he says. "No." I say. "Because…" and we smell beans. And then we see prison workers with rakes, raking leaves near the wire fence and we see prison camp workers stirring huge vats of food for the morning breakfast for the last day of hell. Fuck the camel races. "No, no, no." I say." "Yeah, we're going to the tent," says Kial. "Alright boys. Look, maybe I can fit both?" "Look, cheers man. But we're going to bed." And we start walking away from him. He just stands there looking at us walking away like that big foot thing in that film with the guy from Third Rock from The Sun. The prison camp workers are working around us. They just weave around us doing their prison grounds work because this is after all a correction facility. Correcting fucking what? How easy one forgets. We walk down the long dirt road towards our tent, constantly looking over our shoulder. "What the Fuuuuccckk!" says Kial, "I thought he was our friend?" he continues. "Yeah, dude! What the fuck!? He was protecting us all night from that onslaught. Then he turned." "Oh My God! All night. All fucking night. All those repressed gay cowboys all over me. I feel sick. I need a shower. They were so macho. They just wanted to screw us. I can't believe we made it outta there alive." "I know! Fuck I know!" "What the fuck was all that about?" "I don't know. It was like Wake in Fright. Have you seen that?" "No, nah" "Well, maybe don't watch it for a while," says Kial. "My god, man." We get to our tent. The sun is out. It's hot in there. We take an oxazepam each. We go the fuck to sleep.

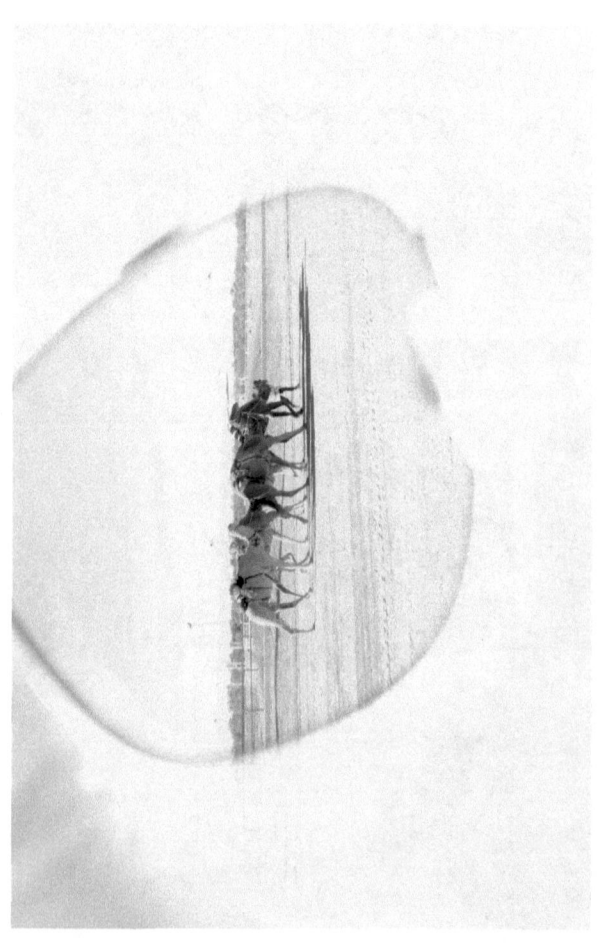

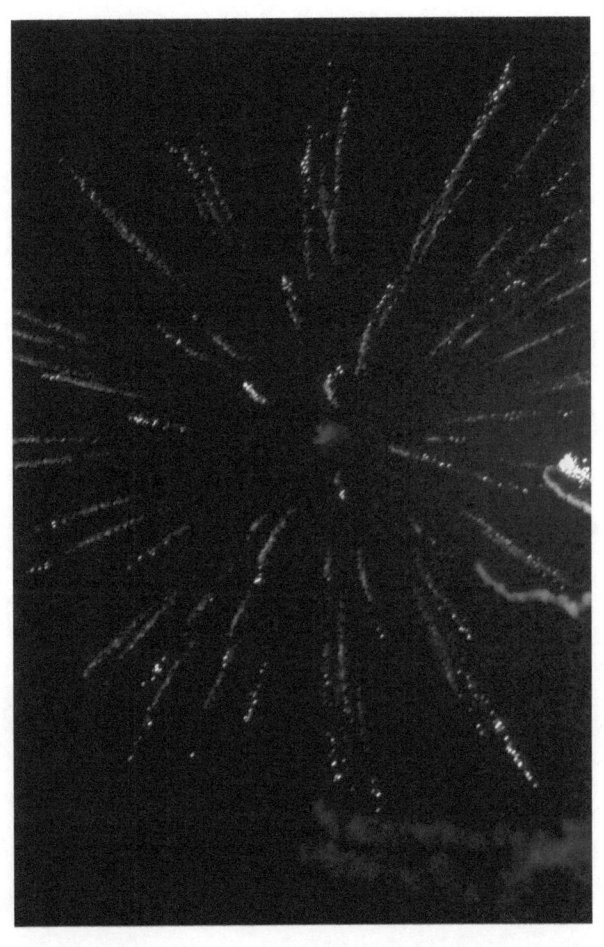

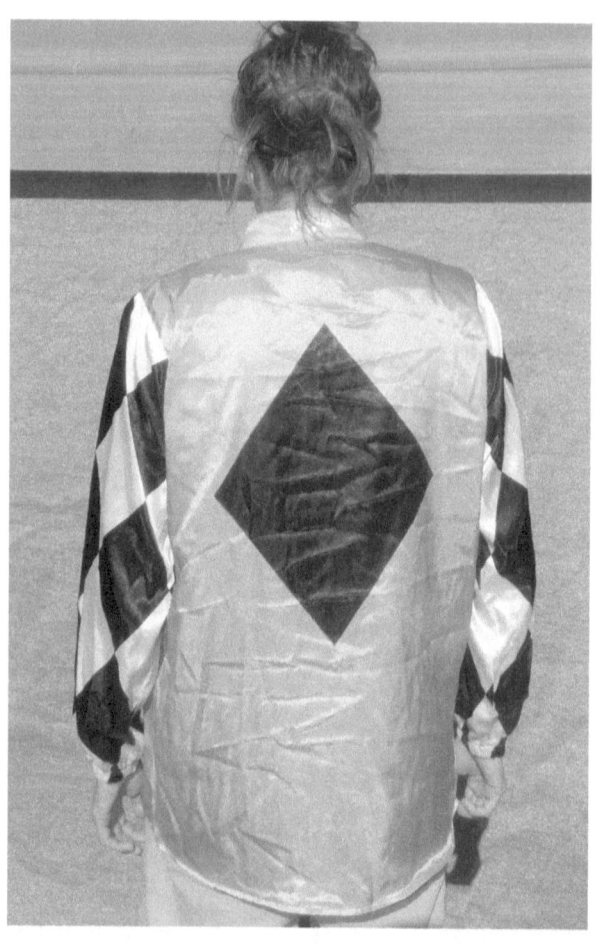

6

I Am Dysfunction

Mid-afternoon and we're nearly steamed alive in our tents. Same thing on both our minds. Words weren't necessary. How. Soon. Can we. Leave. "So, what do we do? I mean, I feel like that speeding fine was a warning. Imagine how shit it'd be if you lost your license!" "Yeah, I'm definitely still over. I'm not driving yet." "I'd drive, but, I'm absolutely still drunk." "Yeah." We say this standing outside the tent. Leaning on the rental in the fucked bright sun. It's as if we parked this car in the middle of nowhere deep dreary dark red wretched fucking hell. All our caravan neighbours with their smouldering fires, meat pie families and snake lunch dogs have disappeared. Somehow, the horror of the past evening seemed to have swept away all the humanity, if you'd call it that. But I guess that's exactly what it was. Humanity. Humanity is the camping neighbours, yes. Also, the camel wranglers, camel racers, canteen ticket stubbers, cowboy gamblers, sexually repressed lurkers, self-escapists, outback truckers, Bundy gulpers, the are-you-a-faggoters, the Goanna Pullers, the glazed-eyed church girls, the wanna-take-a-walkers, the cashed-up cattle-ranchers and King Bitches, the sad gacked mums, the pedos, the horny and unbeknownst teens, the sales reps, the darters, the you-wanna-get-fucked-up-the-assers, the *Rushes*. The damn outback *Rushes*. And us, the maddened documenters of the hellscene and hellscape for what purpose? To find one in our work. Humanity, is, by all means, a fucking nightmare. But you can't sleep through it. The heat wakes you up.

We know we won't find any coffee this morning. We know we won't find any food. Our heavy bones don't want to crack their way back into the race grounds. Not after last night. Tin roof. Concrete floor. Plastic republic. Our still drunk blood was clotting at the idea that we might revisit the grotesque pit. We leaned against the rental. We sat under the ant infested tree. We sat in the car with the air conditioner on. I didn't want to smoke. Somehow, we had two Emus left. "So, we'll wait till you can drive?" "Yeah, I think I don't want to risk it." "Yeah, fair. Do you want me to split the drive home with you? Break it up a bit?" "Nah, nah, it's fine." "Ok, well. Fuck this. I'm having a beer I guess." Kial nods. I open the driver door and pop the boot. There are two Emus floating in warm water in the eski. Ssprfft! It froths up and out the split in the can. It drips down my knuckles. I take a sip. It's fine. It's the best thing here. It's all I have going for me. "I'm not gonna be ok to drive for a few hours, man." "Yeah? Yeah, we drank a lot." "Yeah." Inside the rental, with the aircon on, we see the heat of the living sun burning the dirt and dust around us. The void. A void. Everything under the sun is red. "You wanna go for a walk around the track? Check it all out? Morning after?" I realise now that Kial is in psychopath vicinity. Nothing was captured last night, but in the wake, there might be pieces that signify something. A direct link, a visual metaphor of the mayhem. I know Kial. His bracketing of the events, the now slowly realised events of the entire fucking thing tightrope the line of sanity because of total emotional detachment. I've never known anybody that can separate themselves from their experiences like him. He is the photographer that photographers aspire to be. Naturally, but he's worked hard for that detachment. After the last few days, him shooting, scanning, observing, noting and capturing, he is back. He's returned to the abstract and aloof creature that doesn't live in these moments, but through them like a wormhole from dimension to dimension, from this time now, as we are, as we were, to everything that is fathomably future. My spirit is tender. My emotions are wrought. But you never dismiss a genius because of the dysfunctionality of your own. I am dysfunction. I am a need to be a writer. I am not simply a writer. I came here to make myself through a work.

Through a story. I hate myself. But I love him. Despite my inadequacy, my fallible thoughts and my dirty need to create myself, he still loves me. You could boil and bury us, you could excavate our teeth in a hundred shattered pieces a thousand years on and still one thing will always pair us – push the other one on, through eternity. I need him. I'm no writer without him.

It was some kind of mountain to go back. But we had nothing else to do. I had this Emu to drink, and the other in that eski-slosh in the boot. And fuck this fucking car now, and fuck this fucking campsite. Fuck it all. There was no story. There never was a story. We flew out to the desert to see a camel race that we missed. And I wrote about my fear of not being able to write, not being able to see the story that I'd blindly, childishly, trusted to reveal itself. It was all a failure. A joke on ourselves. A prank neither of us could afford. "Fuck dude, ok. Fuck. Alright, what the fuck is it gonna look like now? In daylight? Erghhhh. Gross." I say. "Yeah, gross. It'll be gross." Says Kial. So, I take my notebook and my tea temperature Emu and Kial locks the rental doors and we kick the dust up on the way back to the gate, to where it leads to the track, to where the track is overlooked by the canteen. Cement floor, tin roof. And like everything looks and feels like today, the grounds are red, the track is red, there's nobody here, at least. At fucking least. But that feeling is red. Dark dark red.

We meander and attempt nonchalance past the carnie rides. There're no food trucks around. The rides look like lies. Weren't they always? We turn the corner when we see the track. We look up the little slope toward that concrete cesspool that hosted the hostility of last night and see all the chairs stacked up neat. All the shutters on the canteen windows bolted. The sinister cement floor hosed down. Through the glare of the earths fucking unquitting star, it all looks normal – it all looks adolescent. It's a tuck-shop between term three and four school holidays. Like the rides, it lies. Like everything we wanted, it lies. Like a fucking story or a photograph, it fucking lies. We duck under the racetrack gate and sit on the hill, ambiguous, silent, stale. And we stare at the shed thing and the canteen. And we stare a while. Then we look at the camel pens, vacant and shat in. We take in the whole view. Hot, half drunk and getting drunker to cope. Thankfully Kial's getting more sober to get us outta here. We sit in the blazing sun, for too long, before we walk back through the cheap abandoned carnival to the car. And when, near silently, we reach it, we screw up the fuckin tent and throw it in a bin down the path. Fuck that tent. Fuck this car. Ergh, I'll keep my sleeping bag. Kial keeps his. But whatever we can bin we bin and I wished he'd just ball me up and throw me in with it after the pegs and the bin bags we bought from Woolworths. I wanted to throw him in the bin too. We deserved to be dumped and illegally shipped out to Asia. We deserved to slowly ferment down to acidic biological matter. Plum sauce. Ketchup. Whatever. And after the driest hottest and most hate fueled pack up, we sat in the car. Kial took a breath. Checked his phone. No reception. I sipped the tepid bathwater beer and we drove into town.

At this point it became alarmingly clear that this country wasn't for us. Kial cautiously steered out the camp site that was now indecipherable from any other red rocky dip or red rocky mound. In our wake was a spectre of depravity and dopamine chasing gamblers and cozily cashed-up docile retirees. In ten minutes, we were in town. Kial pulled over outside what seemed to be an excuse for a house. The only homelike feature being a rotting white picket fence. He restarted his phone over and over, desperate for reception so we could book back into the same motel we stayed in on the way into this hot faggot hating hell. He had no bars. My phone had been dead and useless for days. I got out and fetched the last Emu. I sat back in the passenger seat. Kial leaned outside the driver's door searching for bars. I slurped at the warm shit can. I looked out past him. My skin like teeth. There's a tree covered with white and pink flowers. All in bloom. All horny and happily littered. He gets in. "No good. Fuck." "Oh, dude. I guess, we find some place where we can use a phone then?" "Yeah, I think I remember a payphone." "That feels right." "It does, doesn't it?" He looks out his window at the blooming fertile tree as tall as a powerline. And he says to me, "Are they birds?" "Holy shit! They are, aren't they?" And we stare at them a bit, and some of those flowers flap their petals and fly off their branch, and then other white and pink shaded big blossoms swoop in and take their perch. "Man, yeah! They're fucking cockatoos? Galahs?" "Jesus," says Kial. "I've never seen so many in my life." "Nah, me neither. What the fuck man." And the tirade between branches and swoops continue as we watch from the car, astonished. It was as if the entire tree, three storeys tall was just twigs, branches, sticks and birds. I got that hot Emu down quick then. Something in me needed chaos. Habit by now. It doesn't take much. Had I not had my fill? Further into town we go. There's really one, two, maybe three streets. We pull up to an RSL looking place. They don't sell booze. Or tobacco. Pointless. So Kial asks about their Wi-Fi. They were vague and destitute like the rest of town. Kial couldn't log into their thing and they were doing the, 'you dun luke lark lokal folk' thing. We agreed that they were pricks and reversed out the 45-degree street park, did a loop, and pulled up to a Telstra payphone-booth. We pooled our silver coins together. Luckily, I had the Motel number in my notebook. Kial called them. I sat in the passenger seat for a few seconds until it hit me. This is insane. Kial had the payphone pressed between shoulder and ear, in a dirty dusty white T, too short for him. His jeans straight legged, loose from no food, and reddened by horror. Boots were looking sharp, give him that. Those boots were in their element under the hem of those light blues clopping about a payphone cubicle. I got out the car and filmed his stupid fucking conversation. "Hi, yeah, I'd like to book a room for tonight?" I circled him at 180 degrees, back and forth like a Newton's cradle. "Yeah tonight. Two beds if you can?" "Yeah. Nah. No worries." "Yeah, right? No worries, yeah." "Alright, cheers mate. Yeah, nah. Yep, by 9pm this evening." "No worries. Yep. Alright. Cheers. Yep. Cheers." I don't know what came over me exactly. It could have been any number of things. But Kial in that booth, man, must've been ten years since he'd used one. And his filth. And desperation to get us a room. And the dumb necessity of it. And the dumb necessity of the whole fucking thing. Well, that Emu was done and I was drunk. We gave up on getting travelers in town. More pertinent was petrol and coffee. We pulled into a BP with some trashhole coffee outlet attached. Kial pulled up to the tank and as he did we both looked out the left window at the man shaking the last few drops outta his phallic petrol pump. This man flicked his mullet underneath his cap like a redneck backstreet boy. He squinted in slow motion. Then, without him even glancing in our direction, that's how unobservant and fissured this inch-thick glasses-wearing fiddler was, he limped (yes limped) inside the shitty fucking BP to pay for his fuel and fuck off to what I can only assume to be the nearest family members house with kids under twelve. Here cometh uncle Terry with an oiled fly and greased fingers for the girls. We stared at the bastard. Speechless. I felt in Kial what I felt. I knew we both wanted him to crash and burn. I wanted his skin charred and his flesh sooty. I wanted to see him screaming in a pitch that wasn't vocal. In the high taught noise of air escaping from burning balloons. His campsite-shower drain-pipe lips. I wanted the whole BP, though we were parked right in it, to fucking catch fire. I swear, if you've got an ounce of humanity in you, for bad or for good, you can spot a teenie-taster like that in a quarter-second. He was a grimy sub yanking Kial's sunglasses off his face last night. A sub around men and a pusher round the kids. I can't fucking explain how obviously pedophilic this bastard was. So, me and Kial, we sat in the car a bit, till he left. And we imagined him on fire squealing out oxygen from his pathetic little orifices like a boiling lobster, and we didn't need to talk about it. We just watched him die in our heads, till he left, to go perpetuate more fucked up visions of his own self. He'd create more. More of himself. Parasitic queef. We filled up. Got coffee. And outta Boulia was first priority. And outta Boulia we, well didn't speed, but we went as fast as we could within the speed limit. Right against the signs. 80km? How's 82 all the way?

I knew that racist little bottle stop wasn't too far off. So, I'd have to wait. I was so sautéed from last night that two Emus in the morning had been enough so far. I also had more pressing issues. Kial had a five hour drive ahead, at least, and it was late afternoon. In my naivety I'd assumed we'd get there before nightfall. In my god damn naivety. We drove down the red road to somewhere else, somewhere on the way to home. A place I'd started thinking about a lot that morning. My beautiful partner. This non-monogamy thing was new. Very new. It'd been a week or maybe two since we started. I was excited about it but I was lonely too. I'd had no reception and I knew that when she proposed it a few weeks ago she already had a man set up. I didn't mind. That love could beat anything coming at us. But I had some anxiety about how close we'd feel when I got back. Overriding that was the sincerely infantile desire to be cradled by her. For her to tell me everything was ok. To listen to me verbally puke out all of this. I needed to tell her and explain to her that the outback has a sinister side. If the landscape wasn't enough, Jesus, the men, the women, the red raw eyes and heat. I needed to tell her all of this and I couldn't wait to tell her how it was all a storyless failure. Surely there's some thread in it. I just can't think of it now. I can't feel anything much right now. It sure wasn't the Min Min lights, no, no. It wasn't the Camel racing, no, no. It was something imposturous – insidious – sunken and strangled in a cowboy bathroom. A hair-pulling plonk of the self, of reality, into tepid motel water. Up for air, for a little apprehensive cock, then dunk, dunk, shake, dunk again, faggot. 'Stop breathing,' I could hear them saying. The thing that links all of it is that nothing was what it seemed. Reality was repressed at every encounter. We cruised at the safe speed down the straightest and most bromidic road I'd ever seen. Those faggot hating faggot cowboys. Homophobic homos. I'd feel bad for them if they didn't want to simultaneously beat and fuck us against our will. You want the asshole? Then admit it you bastards!

It feels like 3 hours and we are still only half way to the 'Boong' bottle-shop. Kial wants to pull over cause there's all these cows herding wild through the shit-nothing in our distance. We get out. I smoke. I see a set of white cow bones. I kick em. I squat and twist the dart into the bone and I pocket the butt. I'm not being one of those, I think. I'm not being the white man. And because I am 'the white man,' I don't wanna leave a trace. Just because I am a white man doesn't mean I have to be the white man. This place is the heart of hatred. Kial takes some pics he isn't too enthusiastic about and we climb back in the car. "We far from that town?" "Umm... halfway I reckon." I'm thirsty. And we drive on. And for the first time in a while thoughts of the city are thoughts that feel like home.

Eventually, we reach the racist bottle-shop. Again, they're aggressive, obnoxious, not fond of us. Now it distinctly feels like all the strange looks and all the animosity were because people thought we were a couple. They didn't want a couple of Melbourne poofters in their parts. If we wore Fox racing hats and Rip Curl shorts they wouldn't have batted an eyelid. If you give half a squid's shit about how you look I guess you're a fag out here. Fuck them. Fucking cunts. We get some waters. I get a sixer of XXXX full strength and a four of Bundy and coke even though I can't stand the shit. We get the fuck outta there. "They're fucking cunts in there. What's their deal?" "I dunno, fuck. I just want to get out of here," says Kial. "Maybe this is all adding up? Maybe they figured us to be a couple of gay outback party scene searchers. I mean, they're racist. He is anyway. Safe bet he's a homophobe as well." "Yeah, fuck. Maybe. Feck," says Kial and he twists the key in the rental ignition and I crack a can. "Let's get outta here," he says, head over shoulder reversing whilst clicking in the seatbelt. "Yeah, dude, fuck," I say, and take a real greedy gulp of that XXXX. The can's near gone in two licks. It's gonna be one of those drives, I guess. One of what drives, you might ask? Well, shit, I dunno. Those shitfaced passenger seat drives, long drives. And I figure at this point, if I don't get trashed, he won't make it back. I've gotta keep him aflame. Yeah, I'll get good drunk and I'll entertain him the whole way back. That's my best and only offer and I'm aware of the irony, the falsity, because really, I'm getting fucking drunk no matter what because I'm not driving, and I'm done with thinking and I'm done with observing and taking it all in. There was no good. No good the whole time. It seemed to me that the whole of this section of the vast burnt outback was repressed in all manner of ways. Is repression where evil is cultivated? Denial, selfdom, egoism, narcissism, deflection, suppression? So out of hell we drove, down hell's red dirt road, and I made sure to drink my way outta there just the way I came in.

*
Back To The Abacus

Straight ahead, for how long? Tin after tin for me. But for Kial, it was a dead speedometer settling on 100km per hour and a radio that had no reception on any channel. For what felt like hours, I kept stabbing at the seek button with my index finger. Search motherfucker, search. But nothing. We had fuzz, and white noise crackling and it was as though my attempt to latch a channel was more distressing than just letting the dead noise bleed. So, we bled it. And it hissed and frazzed. Fizzed and fisspped. We aren't out yet I kept thinking. We aren't fucking out. Fuck this landscape and fuck this country. Fuck the depraved mess we were speeding away from. One bad experience, that's all it takes, then the safety switch is on. And every switch on the soul-dashboard was flashing, had been beeping and ringing for a few days. I stuck my head out the window and screamed, "THIS IS OSTRALLLLYA. OSSSTRALLLLLYA. I'M FROM OSSTRALLLLYA. I SPEAAKKKKK OSTRALLLLIAN. OSSSSSSTRALIA. THIS IS OSSSSSSTRALIA!" I screamed in the queerest voice I could muster with my head out the window. I needed a few things. I needed to tell the outback it was fucking gay, because obviously it didn't want to admit it. And I also needed to mock my experience, our experience. Because what the fuck else could I do? And it got Kial laughing and that got me yelling more. And I mocked the whole fucking mentally mangled country. I mocked those fuckers that thought you only get to choose gay or straight, and I mocked those big butthole spreaders that wanted to spread ya if you were a queer, cause you deserved it! I hated the desert. "I'M FROM OSSSS-TRALYAAAA," I screamed more. This isn't fucking ours. And it sure as hell isn't theirs. I swill a XXXX. Am I ignorant of my non-monogamy? I'm in pain. I'm repressing it. Even so, you can't own what you love, because once you do, it'll never be itself. "OSSSTRALLYAAAA!"

There's one XXXX left, there's one can of restaurant sink water. And Kial has been sipping a beer strategically because he's Kial and he isn't me, and that's why I'm not driving, and that's why he is. We cruise, no lane changes, what lanes? Dust and dust and red and red and rust dusty red and red dust. I make a few insipid attempts to joke away this expedition to nowhere and for nothing, and aside from his agreeance in its worthlessness, and the reflectively somnolent organization of what we childishly assumed would be an event, we couldn't squeeze out too much laughter at all. Reality was now the rising moon. And where it had before comforted and consoled in the transition between overture and underture, it now, like the sun, possessed an infernal white ambivalence toward us. Each km brought in the mean moon, closer and closer, each km, dimmer and dimmer. As we drove and drove and drove down one straight line, and as I talked nonsense and slurred my humour all I managed to do for Kial was to stink up the car with the septic reek of booze. The white sedan had become a cockpit of burps, farts and huffs. My alcoholized opinions were now becoming direct avoidances of hallucinations. I stared out the passenger window, the flat-nothing fucking red now blackening space that framed either side of a deadpan apathetic road. And why should it try to carry us, or turn us anywhere? In the descending night it still felt like we were racing out of hell, and we were nearly at the gates, right? No. Not at all. How long has it been? We are alone with the moon, much better than alone with Oafy, but every figure, every symbol felt like a predator. And everything we trusted, the cool air and the stars, became menacing categories of demanding and dominating phenomena. Thank fuck we had each other. Drunk as I was, we knew we had each other. And the moon, or the stars or fucking Mars, would have to get through me first if it wanted Kial gone. And if my time was nearing, as it so often feels it is, he'll be right there, between me and God. "I'MMM FROMMM OSSSTRALLYYAAA" I scream out the window now into the night. And there's still no radio. And we're still listening to fuzz and the purgatory of radio stations for no reason. I notice Kial darting his eyes every now and then to the sides of the empty road. And I know, I see them too. I just hope he isn't seeing what I'm seeing. Because I'm seeing tall dark shadow creatures, 20ft tall, crouching with sinewy limbs behind the shrub. Looming out of the dead dark rocky landscape to snatch at highway grass and open their jagged toothed jaws. Every 500m or so, another and another, and they were long and gangly, and they had no eyes, but they knew we were flying by, and they didn't want us to get to the Abacus. They wanted us dead. The whole planes, the red and now night-swallowed highway, and the absolute goddamn dust - nothing on either side, wanted us to crash. I glanced at Kial each time I hallucinated one of those fucking things. And I saw his eyes, dead straight, an arrow, elbow peeled back perfectly, down the red night highway, bullseye. It must be me. I'm the drunk one. It's me. It's just been a big and sleepless boozed out few days. It's me. It's me. "When did it get dark?" I ask. "I really don't know. I have barely any idea what's going on right now. It's fine. But I keep seeing things." "Weird. It's fine man. That's normal when you've been driving on a single straight road for what? Five hours? How long has it been actually? I thought it took like four hours to get there?" "So, did I. I don't know. This is going forever. I've been having a bit of trouble with my eyes too. Like, focusing, just one isn't as sharp as the other and I can tell. And there's just nothing to keep me alert." "Man, you're doing amazing. This has been fucked and you've barely slept for days. You're killing it. I'm keeping my eyes ahead too, just to be sure. I'm the second pair..." "Yeah, it's fucking weird. My eyesight has always been fine. But recently I've just noticed this focusing thing." "Fuck. And you're a photographer. Well, man, you'll make whatever it is work." "Yeah, just, when your body starts failing you, it just seems dumb. It doesn't make sense. And you try to wrap your head around it. But you can't overcome it because it's physical." "Yeah, I get that. That must fucking suck." "Yeah." "Well, anyway, you're killing it, we must be almost there, surely." And radio fuzzes dumb white noise and we drive in darkness. Nothing but rental headlights, and a road. And I'm seeing the figures, and I'm seeing the shapes, but I can't say anything. Because, its fucking hard enough. And it's not real. If he's driving, I have to be here for him, to collect him, to keep him attached to the straight red line that he is on, for how long… I wish we knew. Still no reception and pop! Fucking roos start darting out in front of us. And Kial slams the brakes. We look at each other with blood-burst eye yolks and the roos stare us down in the middle of the red night road, lit only by a cadence of stars and the shit-shine of our headlights. And over and over they bounce in front of us on our way. So, Kial drives slow and swerves well when he needs to. And the whole way, they just keep plopping out like cute little shits from the asshole crevice of hallucinated shadows fingering at us from the sidelines of the road. Everything is another form of hell. And we have no notions of success other than getting home.

There's a bend ahead, Kial cleans it without the roos. We see lights, some buildings or mines, construction, I dunno. It doesn't matter. There's a society here. It's 8:15pm. The Abacus closes at nine and we still have no reception so we can't call or contact to find out what happens with the keys or if anybody is there to hand them over. More lights. "This is it. We're like 20 away." I say. It's a dead-set lie. "Yeah, we're nearly out!" And that's how it feels, and it's not twenty minutes. It's 45 when we pull into the Abacus. It's so familiar and a haven straight away. The lights are off inside reception. Fuck. I jump out the car and yank the door open. "Hello? Hey?" A recognizable face, the chip server comes to the desk. Suddenly he feels like a friend. "Hey, Kial?" "Urgh, yeah." I say. "I was just bout to close up. Didn't think you were coming." "Shit, man. Ok, well thanks." He passes me the keys, "Room (fucking whatever it was)." "Thanks man. Hey, you still selling drinks?" "Uh, yeah. Just those in the fridge there." Kial walks in. "Hey mate." "Hi," says the desk-boy and I say, "I'm getting drinks," to Kial. "Yeah, sure." He gives no fucks about anything now. I see it. We made it. He's exhausted. He's in some internal way, fucking furious. He's done. We are out of hell. But, this isn't heaven. And he wants home. He wants his girlfriend. He wants his bed. His fireplace. His shower. His toilet to shit in. "I'll grab two six packs of XXXX full strengths." "No worries." And they cost me $28 each and I don't fucking care. I mean, obviously I do. But, it's hard to put a price on contentment now.

Kial's parked already. We lug our bags in but don't unpack. Everything is filled with red dirt anyway. But there's two beds in this room. Two double beds and there's brown brick walls and a television that we might watch. We can't tell. We dump our shit. We sit out the front of our doorway at a small circular table on two wobbly chairs. I roll a cigarette. The six packs are on the table. We don't bother with the fridge. They're going in quick and coldly. And we're gonna mope together about the insignificance of our journey, and the debate, not just with each other, but ourselves, about whether it could possibly turn out to be worthwhile. Every debate with each other is just a debate with ourselves anyway. We drink and we can't figure out whether this experience was worth having. Were we better before? We feel deaf, maybe from the white noise on the radio that bruised our eardrums on the 700 hour long drive back to the motel or maybe because of all the darkness, all of the sun, all of the dirt, or all that syrupy Bundaberg Rum. We couldn't hear anything being said. It was all anguish. And the cold beers were relief. But we weren't out yet, though we were no longer in hell. We were somewhere in-between. And we'd sleep ok tonight. Just ok. That was good enough.

7

Stayin' Alive In Channel Country

At a very AM hour, we shower, dress, pack the rental, drive to the Mt Isa airport or landing strip, whateveryou want to call it, dish off the keys, dump our luggage to go direct to Melbourne, sit like seedy and small people, inconspicuous as possible in a row of a plastic chairs. I think they have two terminals? It's tiny. And we're reminded very quickly that COVID exists. That's right, masks, that's right, sanitizer, that's right, being glared at like you're a host from every stranger in your vicinity. Yesterday, during the drive, and last night by the table out front of the motel, we discussed a lot the feeling it might be like to be a woman, or a young girl, outnumbered by men. To feel like prey. And women experience it day to day, at the supermarket, jogging, at a restaurant, a bar, a club, name a place where these dualities of genders meet and you'll find men overpowered by chemicals in their bushy little ballbags. You'll find everywhere that the mind of man is unwillingly subdued. That glimpse, just a small glimpse into what it's like to be sought, body possessed and claimed, the aggression, the certain demand of you made gestured through a wink. We don't understand, but the insight is distilled. That scene, the one we were suffocating in unbeknownst, was a push/shove scenario. It was a big game with everything on the line. We were on the wrong field. I mean, we were on the field we chose, and we thought we could dodge it all. And we did, we dodged all of the sub assumptions and really, there weren't many options for us to dom. Wait, no, Camel Breath wanted bottom. Open shirt 18-year-old wanted bottom too. But the rest, man oh man. What's the difference? A friend of ours before going to prison expressed his sentiment. It was 'rape or be raped.' And I'll never forget that. It was all a temperature test with them. A fight. A confrontation, then a grapple, then after that… well that'd be it. And I guess that was their gamble, that was their roulette. Anal roulette. So, sitting on the plastic chairs at Mt Isa airport, fairly silent, apart from the occasional moan or agreeable and mutual complaint, we both thought about women and we tried to understand. We understood now better than last week. But in that concrete canteen it was rape or be raped. Somehow, we parried all the punches. Our plane was about to board. We could nearly, almost, not smell the smoldering buggery still emanating from Boulia hell. On the plane. Once we're on the plane, all will be ok.

Board. Short flight. I sleep. Near instantly. Kial no. We depart and the rusty arid landscape drops away. It slides off the edge of the earth, or at least, I was hoping it would. And as I saw it slide, and as I imagined it disappearing forever, I slide off myself, into a deep airplane sleep. I'm good at that. Put me on a moving thing, and I'll pass out. That plane lulled me gently like a child into Brisbane, then suddenly we were there amongst more and more COVID protocols, and sanitations, and masks, and nervous enemies. At least this was clear, everyone was the enemy to everyone else. It wasn't a dom/sub, master/slave virus. It was just a virus. But even in Brisbane airport we asked each other, "were we outta hell?" We didn't feel like it. Just another variation from one hell to the next, and we're just trying to stay alive at this point, not tip over, not miss our flight, stay nourished, hydrated despite faculties vacated. We go to the food court ramen place we went to on the way here, that's the thing people do. They go back. Well, we did. Return to what was normal. And we ordered the same, but it was no good. This time it was tasteless. Everything coming back was harder, longer, more laborious, flavourless and unsatisfying. We had 8 hours in Brisbane airport. So, I drank. Kial and I drank. But I was running out of money and I had to really think about each thing. Each beer now. Reality. Not outta hell, but now infused with reality. For eight hours we shuffled through a few spots to drink beer and we didn't have much to say to each other. It was a continuous shake of the head, a deep sigh, a vague yet unconvincing groan of relief. We made it out unharmed, unscathed, at least physically. That time at the airport, was yet again, another version of hell. There was nothing to enjoy. We sat. We spent money. We drank. And we waited. When we finally boarded the flight back to Melbourne it was as though we'd got a waft from the other side. Things just might be looking up. It's all good. In no time we'll be with our lovers. We'll be held. We'll be kissed. We'll be told we're loved by lovers we love back. And tomorrow will be a new day. And things will make more sense. These days in the desert won't feel how they feel right now. When we board I look out the window clutching *A Fan's Notes*. I can barely bring it up to my dry burnt eyes. And like always, I fall straight to sleep.

Tullamarine, midnightish. Kial's car is in the airport paid parking. We stand at the carousel and the masked figures on our flight, fat-faced strangers collect their luggage and we just stand there watching the empty conveyer belt convey nothing. Nothing anymore. Nothing for us. No bags. "What the fuck man? Are you kidding?" It feels so painfully natural now. Then I see the damaged baggage claim section. There were two bags. Kial's and mine. The rest of the passengers we flew with have left. There's nobody left in this section, at this time, at this desolate airport. Kial's bag is open but more or less together. Mine is wide open, zip broken, clothes flopping out, socks loose. "This makes perfect sense," I say. "Yeah, doesn't it," says Kial and he smiles. I didn't think I had one in me until I saw his. I couldn't zip my bag up. It was fucked. Kial and I walked to the escalator. "Well, I gotta go up to the pick-up point. Fia's texts are looking a little frantic, I think she's doing another lap." "Damn. You good?" "Yeah," I say. "Well, that was something. Maybe nothing. Who knows." He says. "Yeah man, I guess… I dunno. Surely there's something in there. Not what I thought." "Didn't see that turn coming." "Nah, fucking hell. I guess… yeah. It's that story now. Dunno how the photos will reflect all that." "Neither, but going over them on the plane, it's actually all really clear. Almost stupid we didn't see it coming." "Yeah, fuck. Well, I love you man." "I love you too." We hug, tight, and we kiss each other's stubbly cheeks. And I go up the escalator, and he walks out the doors.

He had to get a shuttle bus to his car. He was the only passenger. It was raining. He got to his car. And he drove an hour home, pat-pat-beating wet-ass rain slapping against his windshield. A sad drive.

I called Fia. I asked her where she was. She couldn't explain or I couldn't understand. She was frantic. She was anxious. She was freaking out driving around the airport in the dark and in the heavy rain. The flights were all being cancelled due to more COVID restrictions. I told her to pick me up from domestic. She was unclear. I rolled and lit a cigarette outside. I wasn't undercover. The rain pissed in my open bag. I shielded my cigarette and kept my notebook and my laptop safe. Eventually I get another call. She's downstairs by the bus stop. "Ok, ok. I'll be there in a sec." Wetted, I go back into the airport, I go downstairs. I exit the airport. I cross the road. I walk up and down trying to call her. After a few minutes more in the rain I get through and she pulls up. She's panicking and pulled over. I put my pond of a bag in the boot. She tells me to hurry. To put it in the back. To get in. Get in. I do. "Hey. Fuck, that whole thing was so intense. I don't even know what to say. "Sorry, mum was calling. Where were you? I said to meet me out front of the Royal!" "I was at domestic." She bites her lip and she leans her body into the steering wheel, her face is 10 cm from the windscreen. "How do I get out of here?" "Just go down there. Hey? Hey! I love you." "I love you too. Oh my god, I hate driving around the airport!" "Yeah, it's shit." And she drove me home. And we went inside our house. And I took another oxazepam. And I showered. And I slept like a motherfucker. And the first thing I did when I woke up was start writing. There was something in this after all. I didn't have to search. It wasn't what I wanted or what I expected. I was brittle. But I wrote with a good bottle of wine all day. And I kept writing with a good bottle of wine two days after the first and then I couldn't write anymore. Until now. And now it's done. And what is it about? It's about *Stayin' Alive in Channel Country*.

Originating as a year-long immersive project in the small town of Daylesford, Victoria in 2016: A Stayin' Alive Odyssey is the lifelong partnership of writer James Podhordecki and photographer Kial Menadue. Conceived as a series of Odysseys, the pair have carved out a unique collaborative style - Aussie Gonzo Existentialism.

www.ingramcontent.com/pod-product-compliance
Lightning Source LLC
Chambersburg PA
CBHW031414290426
44110CB00011B/375